LIFE CYCLE
OF A
NEW
CONGREGATION

LIFE CYCLE OF A NEW CONGREGATION

FLOYD TIDSWORTH, JR.

Foreword by Charles L. Chaney

BROADMAN PRESS

NASHVILLE, TENNESSEE

4260-69

ISBN: 0-8054-6069-1
Library of Congress Card Catalog Number: 92-21633
Printed in the United States of America

Library of Congress Cataloging-in-Publication Data

Tidsworth, Floyd, 1932-
    Life cycle of a new congregation / Floyd Tidsworth, Jr.; foreword by Charles L. Chaney.
    ISBN 0-8054-6069-1
    1. Church development, New. 2. Parishes. I. Title.
BV652.24.T48   1992
254'.1—dc20   92-21633
                                            CIP

CONTENTS

FOREWORD

Life Cycle of a New Congregation takes church planting beyond the birth of a congregation to its maturity and into the process of continuous reproduction.

It is a book that can be extremely valuable to several groups of people.

Many lay people have no idea what church planting is or why there is need in America for new churches. The announced goals for new churches by the end of the century among all denominations in North America exceed 55,000. Most denominations have a century-end strategy for new church development. Lay leaders are asking "What?" and "Why?" This book is a brief introduction to church planting from a holistic perspective. Church planting is not splitting up a church and having different groups meet in different places. Church planting is more like the natural growth of a family through children, grandchildren, and great-grandchildren. This book helps people see church planting from the perspective of joy.

Life Cycle of a New Congregation is a book to be passed around among lay leaders and placed in church libraries. It should be required reading for Missions Development Councils, Missions Committees, Deacon fellowships, and other decision-making groups in your church.

Second, this book should be read by students of church planting and church growth. It serves as a practical though brief introduction to the larger goals in church planting—(1) a vigorous group of believers, united in Jesus Christ, led by the Holy Spirit, and honoring God with their lips and lives; (2) a functioning congregation able to make disciples from the world and build new believers that become responsible members of His church; and (3) an effective church able to reproduce itself in its own or another culture.

The book provides a more traditional model for church planting, the model that will be used in most of the congregations started in the next quarter century. The book does not suggest that this is the only model. There is no "one and only way" to start a church. Floyd Tidsworth heads up a division of work that attempts to start churches every possible way. This book provides a process that is basic to all church starts. It is a beginning point in the study of church extension.

Finally, the book should be read by church planters, pastors of sponsoring churches, and church extension professionals. Floyd Tidsworth is not only a student of church planting methodology, he is an experienced veteran of the church planting process. He has planted churches, supervised church planters, and managed people who manage church planters. He is familiar with the work of others in the field. He knows his subject academically and experientially.

This book will prove a practical help to many.

Charles L. Chaney
Vice-President,
SBC Home Mission Board, Extension

ACKNOWLEDGMENTS

My first word of gratitude is to God who provides relationship with Himself, and who makes fruitful church planting possible.

One of His greatest blessings has been the people along my new-work journey. Many have coached, inspired, and provided opportunity for the exercising of gifts. I shall always appreciate Andrew Hall, John Snedden, Thomas Halsell, Jack Redford, Charles Chaney, and Larry Lewis.

A special word of appreciation goes to the New Church Extension Division staff and missionaries of the Southern Baptist Home Mission Board who keep me updated on church planting. Reid Coons deserves special credit for the days of professional editing she gave to this book.

DEDICATION

To Mary Ida, Connie, Mark,
and my extended church planting family
with whom we have served in churches,
missions, associations, and state conventions.

INTRODUCTION

One of the joys of parenthood is watching our children progress through the stages of the human life cycle. God presents us with a helpless infant. Before a year passes, the child enjoys "peek-a-boo." At age three or four he likes to share with other children. From ages seven through eleven he prizes clubs, comics, and computer games. As an adolescent, the child begins to develop his life values and struggles with implementing those values. Finally, adulthood arrives and he assumes responsibility for himself.

Delightful and difficult times accompany each stage of child development. The mother of one hyperactive child told her pastor that she considered following Hannah's example and leaving the child at the church (see 1 Sam. 1:28). Some events in our children's teen years remind us of the "dumb" things we did as teens.

Each stage in the life of a child has a purpose. Developments in one stage prepare a youngster for the next phase.

In the providence of God, new congregations also move through identifiable stages from infancy to adulthood. Full development within each stage builds a strong base for a vigorous "adult" church.

Rodney Napier and Matti Gershenfeld say, "Groups, like individuals, develop through predictable stages of growth over time. A predictable pattern of group evolution emerges in which each stage has certain definite characteristics."[1]

The majority of new congregations become established and survive. However, some falter or fail. I have observed that plateaued or dead congregations skipped over or bogged down in some phase of development. Solid progress through each developmental stage is vital for growth into a strong adult church. Timing in developmental stages may overlap or be compressed.

Understanding stages in the life cycle can help in church planting. First, it can lead to more rapid and healthy growth of a new congregation. Knowing the hindrances to growth at various stages can assist leaders in overcoming them. Recognizing positive keys through stages can speed growth.

Second, awareness of developmental stages can reduce the loss rate of new congregations. Thirty-six percent of Southern Baptist mission congregations do not become constituted churches.[2]

Third, application of this material on developmental stages will greatly reduce the number of young churches that plateau.

Most healthy congregations progress through six stages of development—discovery, preparation, cultivation, fellowship, mission, and church. Personal involvement in twenty new congregations and observation of hundreds of others convinced me that the most effective churches followed the pattern described in this book. Specialized congregations such as those in senior adult communities may not start and develop by this pattern. Developmental patterns in ethnic, language, and African-American churches may also vary.

The Biblical Pattern

Observable stages of development appeared in the establishment of the New Testament church. Christianity began with one person, Jesus Christ.

Jesus chose and trained twelve men to follow Him. Jesus and the apostles ministered and preached to the multitudes. After the resurrection, the Holy Spirit empowered the congregation of about 120 believers who had gathered in the upper room to pray and select another officer. At Pentecost, a church in Jerusalem was founded with 3,120 members. The new church added additional workers to meet the needs of the many kinds of people in the congregation (see Acts 6).

Then the life cycle began again. Philip went to Samaria to proclaim Christ (see Acts 8:5). Peter traveled to Caesarea (see Acts 10:24). Scattered believers began a new body of Christ in Antioch. The Jerusalem church sent Barnabas to check on the new group (see Acts 11:20-22).

The Antioch congregation, sensitive to the leadership of the Holy Spirit, commissioned Barnabas and Saul (see Acts 13). A string of churches developed from their missionary efforts. The Jerusalem church experienced the joys and pains of producing "children" and "grandchildren" to the glory of the Lord.

Stages in the Life Cycle

In the early days of my church planting experience, some events in new congregations baffled me. For example, the original family of a new congregation left the church after several new families joined. I could not understand such a decision.

Later, my study of the development of organizations revealed that such a response commonly occurs. Reading, listening to many church planters, observation, and experience convinced me that new congregations go through identifiable stages in a normal life cycle.

This book elaborates these stages. Size, age, organizational structure, and group dynamics, as related to the growth of a young congregation, are discussed. Keys to progress through the stages appear throughout the text.

Techniques for cultivating essential elements in each stage may vary. But whatever approach is used, full developmental growth at each stage produces a healthy adult church.

A church may not move through all of these stages. But like a child who misses part of the lessons of life, the church will probably need to go back at some point to capture its missed development. This book identifies the maturation needed during each stage.

Heredity and environment influence progress of a child through the life cycle. A cluster of general factors also affect the life cycle of a congregation. These common determining elements are discussed in chapter 1.

FACTORS THAT AFFECT THE LIFE CYCLE 1

Earth's environment concerns all who reside here. Dale A. Miller of Sandoz Crop Protection Corporation says, "The biological revolution of recent years offers us a way to meet the public's and our own growing environmental expectations."[1] He tells of genetically engineered tomato plants that fend off destructive caterpillars without insecticide sprays. Biotechnology and other disciplines strive to solve Earth's environmental problems.

Just as environmental factors may negatively impact the natural world, there are factors which may destroy the church planting environment. And other factors will build a healthy climate for growth. Before discussing the stages of new church growth, I want to discuss some factors that have a direct impact on the heredity and environment of a new congregation.

The Theological Factor

Founding a new congregation is the work of the living God (see Matt. 16:18). God amazes us with His dynamic activity. The Holy Spirit may not always follow the pattern suggested in this book. All who plant churches should keep uppermost in their minds the basic theological principle that Jesus founded the church. He said, "Upon this rock I will build my church" (Matt. 16:18). The concept of the church is not a denominational promotion plan. The idea of the church came from the mind and heart of God.

15

Jack Redford says, "The Holy Spirit is the catalyst—the energizer—in church planting; he is as basic to establishing new churches as he is to all that the church is and does. Without him, nothing would happen—no desire, no prayers, no answer."[2]

"Methods alone, even correct methods, will not produce a New Testament church. The mechanics of proper procedure must be accompanied by the dynamics of apostolic power."[3]

"New churches are born . . . because the Holy Spirit of God is still at work in . . . [the] world. Indeed, apart from the work of the Holy Spirit there would be no new churches.[4]

Before leaving this world, Jesus said, "Ye shall be witnesses unto me both in Jerusalem, and in all Judaea, and in Samaria, and unto the uttermost part of the earth" (Acts 1:8).

Charles Chaney points out that the Bible refers to the *ekklesia* or church in several ways. (1) *Ekklesia* refers to the *laos* or the people of God, (2) the local assembly convened for a specific purpose, and (3) the *soma* or body of Christ. Christ has purified the *ekklesia* of God. It is a manifestation of Jesus in the world. (4) *Ekklesia* is also the *koinonia* or fellowship of the Spirit.

Chaney says, "Through the process of church planting, the body of Christ is brought to its fullness" (see Eph. 2:11-22).[5]

The apostle Paul knew that God alone actually plants churches. Paul said, "I have planted, Apollos watered; but God gave the increase" (1 Cor. 3:6). Only God can bring conviction to a lost person, inspire people to be involved, and give spiritual gifts to Christians.

Therefore, being in step with God is the church planter's first consideration. Prayer should saturate the whole effort of starting a church. We follow Jesus' commission to take the gospel to all of the world.

Henry Blackaby emphasizes finding out what God is doing, then joining God in His activity. He says, "As God's creation, we [are] on mission with Christ in our world, for the Father's redemptive purposes."[6]

Another theological factor based on scriptural example is that church planters made the gospel very clear to those whom they sought to reach. After hearing an explanation of the gospel, some people followed Christ. Acts 17 records Paul's explanation of the gospel to the Athenians. At the end of his speech, "some men joined him and believed" (Acts 17:34, RSV). Paul and other missionaries started churches with people from all kinds of backgrounds. Some were God-fearers out of the Jewish worship tradition. Others were pagans. No doubt, some had no religious background. All were welcomed as learners or seekers of the Way. But it was necessary to state theological truths clearly to them.

The church planter needs to spend time with the core group of people who will lead in beginning a church. If the core group comes from a sponsoring church, the assumption may be that all are Christians. The church planter should confirm this assumption through core-group Bible study and testimonies. A Bible study group excels as a way to lead people to believe in Christ and/or to mature in the faith.

After conversion, believers need to "grow in grace, and in the knowledge of our Lord and Savior Jesus Christ" (2 Pet. 3:18). When three or more people become members of a new congregation, discipleship training should begin. In Matthew 28:19-20 Jesus instructed us to make disciples, to baptize the believers, and then to teach them to obey His commands.

The core group of a new congregation needs sound theological foundations. They need to be taught the biblical basis and character of the church. They need a growing relationship with Jesus Christ through prayer and Bible study. They should live Christ-like lives that earn community respect.

Another theological truth is that a new church becomes the "body of Christ" in a new location. "And the Word was made flesh, and dwelt among us, . . . full of grace and truth" (John 1:14). Philippians 2:5-7 (NIV) instructs us, "Your attitude should be the same as that of Christ Jesus: Who, being in very nature God, did not consider equality with God something to be grasped, but made himself nothing, taking the very nature of a servant, being made in human likeness."

The Time Factor

Some young friends of ours applied to adopt a child. Because they did not know the age their adoptive child would be, they could not make many preparations ahead of time. One day, they received the news that their baby would be available the next day. Friends contributed necessary items and the new parents brought the little girl home. Biological parents have more time to make preparation for a child's arrival.

In church planting, time factors can be scheduled to provide the best developmental potential. Time has a great influence on the growth of a new congregation.

The first time factor has to do with sponsorship. A congregation discovers where a new church is needed and then considers becoming a sponsor. The church needs plenty of time (from one to six months) to consider sponsorship. If the process is rushed, the church may feel pushed into sponsorship against its will. In some cases sponsorship may be the pastor's idea without the church's support.

On the other hand, if the process continues for more than six months, the momentum for the new start may be lost. The church needs to make a decision about sponsorship while the information is fresh in members' minds.

A second important time factor relates to the cultivation stage. Ministries, community events, visits, and other cultivation activities catch the community's attention. Within two months, these activities should be linked to the beginning of Bible study groups. The community should understand that cultivation activities and Bible study groups are part of the groundwork for a new church.

Third, a mission fellowship or Bible study group will probably need between two and eighteen months to develop into a solid core group. A Bible study group may crystallize and fail to grow unless a steady stream of new people is coming in. A group's growth usually levels off at about eighteen people. The longer a group stays together, the more difficult it is for new people to join.

Peter Wagner points out that a small group or a small church may develop "koinonitis," fellowship gone bad. A group may crystallize and become so comfortable that newcomers find it difficult to become members. The group would probably say they want to include anyone, but their actions may discourage others from joining.[7]

David Putman suggests that the core group be a church planting team. He says that even when the team is from the sponsoring church, it should spend eight weeks together before starting a new congregation. This gives time for bonding without losing momentum.[8]

A fourth time-related factor is the mission launch. Launching a mission too soon hinders a new congregation's growth. The sponsor needs preparation. Workers must be properly oriented. Eager sponsors should be careful to lay solid foundations in the church and in the community before the launch date. Community awareness is a major factor in the birth of a church.

If a new congregation must develop relationships with its sponsor and the community after it is launched, outreach and growth may be hindered.

J V Thomas says the first four months in the life of the mission is the time to reach, win, and develop members. In two to three months, the first members become the second wave of growth leaders. The next four to twelve months are spent getting ready to walk. Expand the organization's growth potential with a ratio of one worker to eight people. Thomas says "the growth process is twofold—making disciples and leading disciples to know how to make disciples." Thomas believes the character of the church is formed within the first two years and changes little thereafter.[9]

A fifth important time factor is in purchasing property for the new church. Some new congregations never buy land. Others need a building site in order to achieve recognition in the community. A careful identification of the target group will reveal the right choice.

Some churches should never consider buying property or constructing a building. Property and buildings could be hindrances to some predominantly mobile congregations. In some locations where construction and property are expensive, wise stewardship might indicate putting money into programs, ministries, and missions rather than buildings.

Rental facilities in shopping centers can become temporary or permanent meeting places. Community buildings may be available for congregations. Saddleback Valley Community Church in Orange County, California, has proven that moving or even meeting in several different locations can be positive success factors. Saddleback Church has continued to grow during the past eleven years while meeting in several different school buildings.

In some cases, churches purchase land too soon, buying what is affordable. Purchase of a small site can inhibit future growth. A wise congregation waits until it can afford the most suitable property.

Other communities, especially small towns, view a congregation's property purchase as its intent to be permanent. If feasible, a sponsoring church should arrange for property purchase before beginning this type congregation. Otherwise, it should set a target date for property purchase within six months, if possible.

In some growing suburbs, early property purchase while choice sites are available is a good investment. Property prices usually escalate as population increases.

The last timing factor relates to constituting a mission into a church. A mission that constitutes before it has members, money, and maturity will be weak. However, if it waits too long to become a church, it may become a dependent congregation. (See chapter 7, "Considering Constitution," for guides to constitution time.)

A church-planting paraphrase of Ecclesiastes 3:1-8 might read:

There is a time for everything, and a season for every activity under
   heaven:
A time to sponsor and a time to prepare to sponsor,
A time to cultivate and a time to speak of the cultivator,

A time for fellowship and a time to enlarge the group,
A time to launch a mission and a time to refrain from launching,
A time to purchase property and a time to meet without ownership,
A time to function as a mission and a time to constitute.
God has made everything beautiful in its time.

The Group Factor

Understanding three broad groupings—cell group, core group, and congregation—can help church planters provide a healthy environment for new congregations.

In plant and animal life, the cell is a small functional unit. It has a nucleus surrounded by protoplasm.

The **cell group** is the smallest organized group in church life. It has a primary leader (nucleus). It may reach up to forty people but still functions as a unit. Everybody may participate in each activity and decision. Many family chapel churches are one-cell groups. The longer a cell functions, the more difficult it is to divide.

The **core group** is larger than the cell. It has more than one primary leader. It is multicelled.

The core group is important to a new congregation. Skills and gifts for leadership toward future growth come from this group. The people who make up the core group determine who the church will likely reach. The core group attracts people like itself.

The third major group is the **congregation.** In reality, a congregation may be large or small. However, for our consideration, it is larger than the core group. It may include attenders who are on the fringe of church life. Several cell groups may exist in the congregation. The congregation is very loosely knit. Within the congregation, everyone is not necessarily acquainted with all others.

The Size Factor

One size church is no better than another. Some people prefer a small church; others respond to a large church. America needs churches of all sizes to provide options for people.

Lyle Schaller says, "One fourth of all Protestant congregations on the North American continent average fewer than thirty-five at the Sunday morning worship service. At least one-half average less than seventy-five."[10]

Some church groups may never develop beyond the cell group in size or nature. Yet, they serve a good purpose. Congregations are needed in apartment complexes and high-rise buildings.

Some church settings and people groups call for mega churches. Other people prefer mid-sized churches. Any size church is a good size if it reaches people for Christ and carries out the Great Commission.

Carl F. George reports that half of the churches will mature at less than 75 worshipers; 80 percent will have fewer than 200; and 5 percent will exceed 750 in worship.[11]

Size is a church cycle factor because a new congregation's starting size affects its growth pattern. Schaller says, "The decision to begin small is consistent with the approach of the pastor who prefers to concentrate on one-to-one relationships with individuals and who conceptualizes this as a collection of eighty people."[12]

Growth becomes limited because the pastor can contact only a limited number of individuals. Leaders in small congregations also think of the group as a collection of individuals. A new congregation that starts with fewer than fifty people runs a greater risk of remaining a one-cell group.

A small beginning seems to attract people who like small churches. When these people become members of a congregation, they hinder numerical growth.

Launching a church when the core group is larger than fifty has some advantages. A study by the Research Division of the Home Mission Board of the Southern Baptist Convention indicates that 43 percent of 526 new congregations that started with fewer than 50 people did not report any activity after 5 years. Of 582 churches that began with more than 50 people, only 16 percent reported no activity after 5 years.[13]

In September 1990, I attended the first service of Roswell West Baptist Mission in Roswell, Georgia. Four fellowship groups had met since July. Through a telemarketing project, group members placed more than thirty thousand calls to local residents. Attendance at the first service was 340. Since then, attendance has been consistent at about 150.

People attend church primarily because they are invited by a relative, neighbor, friend, or associate. A larger beginning group has a greater field of natural prospects.

Dependable families may move away from a new congregation. The larger-sized congregational start has reserves to survive such a loss.

Supporting groups such as sponsors or denominations tend to decrease their support after a certain length of time. A congregation that starts large enough has a good chance for growth and subsequently the ability to assume its own financial support. The congregation with financial resources for programs that meet the needs of the community has a better chance to grow.

Would a new congregation have a better start by remaining longer as one or more Bible study groups in order to gather a larger starting group? I think it is wise to do everything possible to build strength before a new congregation is launched. If it "goes public" then dies, starting again in that community will be much more difficult.

However, hundreds of new missions are needed in villages and small towns across America. Some may never be larger than fifty people. And they will perform a much-needed ministry. In fact, according to David R. Ray, small churches are the right size.[14]

Another size determinant is the one-hundred barrier. Many congregations reach one hundred in attendance, drop back, then begin the climb again. Changes must take place in order for congregational growth to continue past the one-hundred mark.

The key to developing beyond one hundred is pastoral leadership. A pastor can usually handle all responsibilities for a congregation of one hundred. To enable the congregation to grow beyond this point, the pastor must equip and involve others. As Peter Wagner says, he must "be willing to shift from a shepherd mode to a rancher mode."[15] The pastor may begin to enlist others to do hospital visitation and many things that are not essentially pastoral actions.

The pastor who thinks of the congregation as a collection of families, classes, choirs, groups, cells, committees, programs, and events can grow a large church. Harry Fowler says, "The pastor must shift from establishing deep one-to-one relationships to establishing group relationships with members."[16]

From the beginning, the growth-oriented pastor adopts a style of leadership that helps people discover and use their gifts. This decreases the possibility of a dramatic change when attendance reaches one hundred.

According to a study in forty-four growing Southern Baptist churches, 75 percent of the pastors moved when the congregation reached one hundred in attendance. Rather than change leadership styles, they moved to other situations in which they were comfortable. In this study, only 25 percent remained with the churches and made the necessary changes with the congregations.[17]

A church's future size might be said to be genetically determined. The determining genes include birth size, relational patterns, pastoral leadership style, size preference of core group, and recognition of financial potential.

Organizational Factors

Three basic stages in the development of a new congregation are start-up, organization, and growth.

Start-up Stage

- Members know one another. The group is very personal.
- Members know and accept the purpose, objectives, and goals of the organization.

- The trust level is very high.
- The group feels it is in control. It makes decisions easily and quickly.
- Most communication is verbal and informal.
- Members are enthusiastically committed to the organization.
- Members accept struggle and sacrifice as a part of being a group member.
- Change is simple.
- The leader or leaders are known and respected. They are given a great deal of latitude without formal accountability.

Organization Stage

During this time new members join the group, and the organization evaluates itself.

- The trust level decreases as new people come in.
- Communication begins to be less verbal, more written and formal.
- The group becomes more structured and organized.
- Decision making is more formal, takes longer, and is more complicated.
- All members may not agree with final decisions.
- Some members begin to feel they are losing control.
- Members may leave the organization at this stage.
- Leaders are tested. Their positions may be affirmed or changed. Others are dropped. New leaders may be added.
- The organization may purchase equipment and enter new facilities.
- More paid staff may be added.

Growth Stage

Most of the process that started in the start-up and organizational stages may continue during the growth stage. By this time organizational adjustments should allow for growth.

- Buildings, budget, staff, and programs become more important.
- This is the time of greatest possible expansion. Organizational enlargement can help accomplish the group's goals.
- The organization can become recognized and accepted in the community.
- The work must be broken down and done by small groups instead of the whole. The organization completes its work through committees and small program assignments.
- The organization strives to include members in goal sharing by giving opportunity for suggestions and input.
- More staff is added.
- Goals may be adjusted to reflect the achievements of the organization. The group may set new goals that relate to the challenges of the future.[18]

Organizational Stages and the Church

Even though the church was divinely conceived and commissioned, it is made up of human beings. The Book of Acts records a very human reaction: "In those days when the number of disciples was increasing, the Grecian Jews among them complained against the Hebraic Jews because their widows were being overlooked in the daily distribution of food" (Acts 6:1, NIV).

James and John asked Jesus to place them next in authority to Him. When the other disciples heard about the request, they were indignant (see Mark 10:36-41). It seems to me that actions in the early church fit human organizational patterns. But a church group can rise above self-centered behavior dictated by the flesh (see Rom. 8:37-38, NIV).

These organizational stages parallel normal development in congregations. Most new congregations begin with the characteristics mentioned in the birth or start-up stage. Members know and trust one another. They can see what is happening and communicate by word of mouth.

The group moves into the organizational stage as new members and new units of work are added. Members are unable to see or hear about everything that happens. The trust level decreases.

When the congregation moves into the growth stage, members must trust small groups rather than the whole church to do research before making decisions. Moving away from person-to-person relationships may cause trauma unless the group is spiritually mature.

Robert Dale presents a visual description of the organizational factor. He pictures a growing congregation on a bell curve. It starts with a dream, goes to beliefs, then selects goals. As the curve reaches its pinnacle, structure and ministry form. It is at that point, Dale says, that the church must redream the dream.[19]

A congregation may need to redream either in the organizational stage or the growth stage. How long a mission or a church has been in a particular stage determines whether or not it needs to redream its dream. The increase of new members is also significant to renewing the congregation's vision and goals.

A congregation that begins to think nostalgically needs to refocus its ministry. When a congregation's beginnings become more visible and talked about than its future and growth, it is a red-flag warning of a possible plateau. Certainly it is time to evaluate where the congregation is and what God wants it to do.

So theology, time, size, social groups, and organization have a bearing on the stage development of a church. Your observation of these factors can help your congregation proceed smoothly through stages of growth.

2 ILLNESSES THAT RETARD GROWTH

When I was ten years old, I broke my arm on the school playground. My teacher helped me get in the car for the trip to the hospital. A group of children gathered around to watch.

At home, Mom gave me a special ice cream treat. I did not have to do my usual chores. But neither could I play as usual.

Parents want to protect their children from accident and disease. Some illnesses last briefly and have no lasting effects. Others are fatal. Still others may slow or permanently stunt growth.

New congregations are especially susceptible to the ailments described below. One illness may cause a baby church to falter. Several ailments at once may bring about church failure. An accurate diagnosis and proper treatment can alleviate the disease. Church planters often observe the following ailments.

Spiritual Anemia

Usually, a new congregation is composed of dedicated Christians. Their high motivation gives them a desire to do whatever is necessary to make the church succeed. But they must beware of the following symptoms of spiritual anemia.

Burnout may develop because of overactivity. Activity is usually emphasized in a new church. The unchurched need visits, the community needs ministry, the meeting place needs volunteer cleaning help, and the pastor needs survey assistance. The number of workers may be small. Staff may be part time. Some members may become burned out and leave the new church.

Church planters may also suffer burnout. I agree with Bruce Baldwin, a psychologist in Wilmington, North Carolina, who says there is a process in burnout. He points to five stages: intimate involvement, exhaustion/questioning, the balancing act, withdrawal/ disappointment, and terminal cynicism.[1]

For church planters, the first of five stages of burnout is the **honeymoon.** It is a time of fresh beginning. Everything looks good. Getting acquainted and developing the work environment claims attention. With church planters this phase lasts from six months to one year. Larry McSwain, referring to a clash between pastor and people, says "The first such skirmish occurs at the conclusion of the 'honeymoon' period of a pastorate. This is three to six months after beginning a new ministry."[2]

The second phase of burnout comes as a result of overinvolvement in work. The church planter becomes worn out. **Exhaustion** may show up in physical and/or emotional fatigue. He may feel that results have not been proportionate to his invested labor.

The third phase is **decision time.** The church planter must decide on the use of time for family, leisure, spiritual, and work pursuits.

If he does not find a balance, the fourth phase will show itself. **Withdrawal** is the usual reaction. He may neglect his work and begin an avocation. Or he may concentrate on one part of the work, such as reading, to the exclusion of the whole job. Confusion may arise at home. Boredom may become a problem.

The last phase is a **feeling of failure.** The church planter then protects himself by getting out of the work. He may become bitter and rebellious toward church planting or the place and people where he worked.

But burnout is not the only possible course. In phase three, decision time, the church planter can decide to manage his life under God. He can determine to balance his time for family, recreation, spiritual development, and work. Hundreds of church planters have succeeded in achieving balance. The usual result is a fruitful ministry in the current location and in the future location.

Spiritual fatigue can occur in small congregations where a few people try to do all the work. Members may succumb to the temptation to neglect personal devotional time. The church may fail to plan quality time for members' spiritual enrichment and nurture.

What is the medication for spiritual anemia? Many new congregations have prevented or cured this illness. How did they do it?

Prevention is always the best medicine. From the beginning, a church should plan for spiritual nurture. Some new churches gear their Sunday morning worship services toward the unchurched. They plan Sunday night services for members' spiritual enrichment.

Many denominations have materials and systems to help new Christians develop patterns of Bible study and prayer. These tools help Christians continue their spiritual growth and develop a close walk with God.

Early in its life, a Chicago church began new-member orientation groups for new converts and those transferring membership. As a result, some veteran church members learned how to study the Bible. They realized the relationship of consistent Bible study and prayer to spiritual strength.

Some new churches use *MasterLife*[3] or another study method to teach members how to relate to Christ, to the lost, and to other Christians. They also teach about the church and world missions.

The goal is to "reach unity in the faith and in the knowledge of the Son of God and become mature, attaining to the whole measure of the fullness of Christ" (Eph. 4:13, NIV).

Cure. A church infected with spiritual anemia may be cured. If the cause is burnout, let up for a time. Jesus withdrew to pray (see Luke 6:12). At the time of the transfiguration, He took Peter, James, and John apart with Him for inspiration (see Mark 9:2). The late Vance Havner said, "If you don't come apart, you may fall apart." This could be true with churches.

A retreat may be in order to deal with any or all of the symptoms of spiritual anemia. Plan time for prayer, Bible study, and fellowship. Invite an outstanding spiritual leader to direct the church in enrichment. Seek closeness to God and renewed fellowship with one another. "By this all men will know that you are My disciples, if you have love for one another" (John 13:35, NASB). Several denominations have retreat planning guides and leaders who can direct a church in renewal.

Continue Christian nurture as a part of the total church program. To replace envy, teach an attitude of service to others in the name of Christ. Give attention to spiritual growth in at least one worship service each week.

Most new churches have small groups for Bible study, sharing and prayer, and affirmation. The groups provide close fellowships of care and concern. The Sunday School meets this need in many churches.

The Grasshopper Complex

The majority of the spies Moses sent to investigate the promised land had a grasshopper complex (see Num. 13:33). Observing walled cities and giants, ten of the twelve spies gave the alarming report that the Israelites appeared as grasshoppers in comparison to the local people.

God had delivered these same people from Egypt. He had shown them many miracles and demonstrations of divine power. God had promised to give the land of Canaan to the Israelites. The spies failed to see beyond their own weaknesses and human limitations. They suffered from lack of faith in God.

It is easy for a new church to compare itself to more established churches that have adequate equipment, many workers, and spacious buildings.

New churches may experience criticism from other churches that do not recognize the need for a new church in their community.

The unchurched world may overwhelm a new congregation. Thousands are in the pagan pool, while a handful are in the church puddle. The world has money, leaders, and organization. Grasshoppers ask, "Can our little church even make a splash in the pagan pool?" Only faith can answer Yes!

The grasshopper complex is a serious disease. Infected church members may jump right out of the new congregation or fiddle away the time and not prepare for days ahead.

Preventing the grasshopper complex lies in a vision from God. Church leaders can help the congregation unite in seeking God's purposes for their church. The congregation may need to refocus its vision. Prayer requests, progress reports, and challenging messages can help keep the congregation's dream in focus.

Cure. A minister in Indiana became the pastor of a congregation with a grasshopper complex. First, he called the people to prayer. Then, realizing that the church needed to be successful in some way, he led the people to adopt a challenging project.

Church members had lost confidence in themselves. Theologically, they believed God could accomplish His purposes. But they questioned, "Could He do it through us?"

Benjamin Reeves said, "The problem with a lot of Christians today is that they are pessoptimists—people who believe everything is going to get better, but it will be too late."[4]

The Indiana pastor gave his grasshopper complex-infected congregation a strong dose of encouragement. Prayer, a successful project, and reassurance overcame their illness. Today the church is one of the outstanding Baptist churches of Indiana.

When this illness strikes, the pastor should resist a critical-sermon approach. Rather, it is time for the "one-minute praising" described by Kenneth Blanchard and Spencer Johnson in *The One Minute Manager*. Catch the people doing something right and praise them for it.[5]

Another curative needed for this disorder is reaffirmation of God's power. "Now faith is the assurance of things hoped for, the conviction of things not seen" (Heb. 11:1, NASB). Praising God is powerful medicine. Prayer is the way we get in touch with God's power. Through prayer, a church relearns what God wants to do through it. Henry Blackaby, director, Prayer and Spiritual Awakening, Home Mission Board, SBC, says of a new church in Canada where he was pastor, "It was not a formula for church planting that was needed, but a Person to follow and trust."[6]

Grasshopper people's negative attitudes toward themselves and their churches deter growth. Unchurched people detect negative attitudes and do not want to board a sinking ship. I heard a grasshopper individual say, "Why visit? Who would want to come to our church?"

Grasshoppers have forgotten that they are servants of the living God. True worship with God at the center can lift the attitudes of grasshoppers about themselves and their circumstances.

The Jewish elders ordered Peter and John "not to speak or teach at all in the name of Jesus" (Acts 4:18, NIV). In response, the early Christians gathered and prayed. They recognized God as the Creator of all things. They would not be defeated by earthly rulers when they served the sovereign Lord of the universe (see Acts 4:24).

The Welfare Syndrome

The welfare syndrome is another ailment that may retard a young congregation's growth. The major symptom of this infectious disease is the attitude that "someone else should support our church." This illness occurs most often in young churches that have received financial resources from their denominations or sponsoring churches. The congregation may have received too much for too long.

Prevention of the welfare syndrome should begin well before a new congregation is formed. Church planters, denominational leaders, and sponsoring churches can determine the potential of proposed church fields. Demographic information on age groups, income and educational levels, marital status, and housing patterns is available by census tract, ZIP code, township, or precinct.

Information about socioeconomic group characteristics, values, life-styles, and behavior patterns within a community is available from companies that do market segmentation for businesses. Refer to *American Demographics*[7] for a listing of these companies.

Demographic information can assist church starters in determining locations for new churches. The statistics can also point to a community's ability to support a church, a building program, and a full-time pastor. Using this information, church starters can plan realistically for a church that meets a community's needs.

Another preventive measure is to establish a planned phasedown of outside support. Methodically, the new congregation can move toward self-support. A young congregation is like a teenager growing toward adulthood. The process of becoming self-supporting should be gradual, but steady.

The best **cure** for welfare syndrome is stewardship development of church members. People who come into a new church can easily see the need for funds. Inform new members of current programs and long-range plans. Display plans for future buildings. The church could escrow funds for future pastoral support.

Bible teaching and preaching on stewardship is healthy for any church. This does not mean just talking about raising money or promoting giving. It means helping people learn to be stewards of every part of life.

If prevention and stewardship development are not effective, radical surgery may be the only cure. Groups supplying financial support may need to notify the new congregation that all support will cease as of a certain date. Sponsors should allow some time for the young church to adjust to its new financial responsibility. A series of minor surgeries or phasedowns over a longer period is desirable.

Consider another approach that has been effective. Church X received assistance from its denomination for twelve years. Leaders challenged the church to sponsor a new congregation in another city and provide $500 each month for the new start. Church X accepted the challenge and after one year, dropped its request for aid from the denomination. Church X continued to give $500 per month for the new church.

Two factors operated in Church X. One was the challenge of a project that needed their help. Church members increased their giving because of need awareness. The other factor was that members became less self-centered. When the congregation began to look beyond itself and give, individual members caught that spirit.

Field Blindness

Field blindness is a contagious malady that most often afflicts older churches. However, a new congregation can become field blind at an early age.

Twentieth Street Mission wanted to be just like its mother church. Workers who came from the sponsoring church wanted to clone their beloved sponsor.

At the end of two years, Twentieth Street Mission was no larger than it had been six months after its start. The people in the community were not like the folks in the mother church. They did not respond to the same kind of music or worship style. The pastor from the sponsoring church was not Twentieth Street community's "kind of preacher."

A consultant did an objective study of the community (field) and diagnosed the problem as field blindness. The new church's leaders then recognized the problem. They had been looking at the mother church instead of looking at their own field.

Twentieth Street Mission rearranged its program and ministry to relate to the people who needed the church. They became all things to all people so that by all possible means they might save some (see 1 Cor. 9:22).

Prevention. A study of demographics or life-styles and values before a mission begins, or early in its life, can prevent field blindness. The sponsoring church can tailor its early plans to the needs of the people it wants to reach.

Cure. In churches where field-blindness infection occurs, the solution may come by looking through new glasses. An objective study of the target area or group will reveal whether or not programs and church leaders meet the needs of the target people. People with field blindness often resist change. To be a healthy, growing congregation, a church must change to meet the needs of the community or group.

Frogitis

Frogitis is jumping too soon. It may happen in relation to a pastor, property, or building construction.

Some eager congregations jump into calling a pastor who is not fitted for their situation. Calling a pastor because he is available or because the church can afford him is seldom wise. The pastor is the primary human key to growth. A congregation should continue an interim position and wait for the best-qualified pastor possible.

New churches may be tempted to jump too soon in acquiring property and buildings. Frogitis often occurs when someone offers the new congregation free land. Adequate acreage and prominent location are factors that must be considered because of their direct relationship to growth.

A third variety of frogitis causes premature jumping into a building program. Undue financial pressures result when congregations assume debts they cannot manage. Pastoral support and church ministries can suffer as a result. The community, aware of financial problems, may respond, "That church just wants us to help pay their debt. No, thank you."

Excessive debt also hinders a second building stage. Some churches succeed in reaching people and filling a first unit. Debts can delay or prevent the addition of other units.

The **preventive** medicine for frogitis is prayerful planning. Mission pastor Farrell Ard and sponsoring church pastor Mark Brooks of Elmdale Baptist Church, Springdale, Arkansas, led committees to make early building decisions. Before having its first Sunday service, the new congregation decided to postpone building until they had reached thirty families and a stated level of local offerings. As the congregation grew, some members were eager to launch into a building program. The pastor and sponsoring church held the new congregation to the earlier decision.

They secured land and developed plans for a first building. When the church reached its goals for member families and local offerings, construction began.

The congregation experienced growth during the waiting period. Enthusiasm was high. Adequate time was available for securing permits and other preparation. The new congregation held worship services in a mobile unit. Two Sunday School classes met in nearby homes.

Although these measures were inconvenient, they were growth activities. The community recognized that the new church was "bursting at the seams." This kind of activity reveals success. Unchurched people are more likely to respond to these conditions.

Cure. If frogitis is taking its toll, self-diagnosis and treatment may be possible. Other churches have found the following procedure helpful.

Determine what percentage of your county's population the churches of your denomination are reaching. It will probably be between 5 percent and 20 percent. Consider that your congregation has potential for reaching 10 percent of the five thousand unchurched people in your church field. You expect the community to grow by one thousand. Only 50 percent of your members will be present for a given service.

$$5{,}000 \text{ unchurched} \times 10\% = 500 \text{ people}$$
$$1{,}000 \text{ new people} \times 10\% = \underline{100} \text{ people}$$
$$600 \text{ potential}$$
$$600 \div 50\% = 300$$

Using this formula, your church would need at least three acres and adequate buildings to minister to three hundred people. The same formula may apply if you work with people groups rather than geographical communities. If your church has only one acre, it may need to move to larger property. If your congregation does not choose to purchase property, the next choice is to start another church within your field.

Another type of frogitis appears when a church has adequate property and buildings but has a staggering debt. In this case, it is wise to engage the services of an adviser who specializes in church finances. Refinancing may be a possibility. A debt-reduction campaign may be the answer. Sister churches or the denomination might make one-time contributions. Doing something is essential. Without care, a patient with frogitis could die.

Chronic Misplaced Priorities (CMP)

Spending time, energy, and finances on nongrowth activities is evidence of a congregation's affliction with CMP. A new congregation can organize itself to death. "If the members become tied to meetings they will not be able to reach people."[8] New churches grow by touching the unchurched.

In the first year of a new congregation's life, the pastor should spend 50 percent of his time on outreach. He has little hospital visitation and counseling to do. Administration is at a minimum. There is no shortcut to contact with people. The new congregation does not have a large number of members to visit the unchurched. It is my observation that a new congregation should spend 10-25 percent of its income on outreach to the unchurched.

Prevention of CMP begins with a basic understanding of growth principles. Each new congregation should consider having a growth seminar to help it develop a pattern of growth thinking. Set priorities based on growth principles.

Cure. New churches infected with CMP may be able to correct the situation by examining their priorities and studying growth principles. Cut out the fat. Get on a strict diet of growth priorities and watch the church shape up.

Churches that cannot face their own priority problems or do not understand church growth principles may need outside help. Church planting or church growth specialists may help a congregation recognize problems and devise a plan for church growth. Each infected church must decide to pay the price of change or limp along with CMP infection.

Doctors tell us to eat balanced diets, get plenty of exercise, and rest in order to stay healthy. I trust your new congregation can start life in a healthy growth pattern.

3 FINDING A MATCH

The Discovery Stage

The custom of dating gives a young person opportunities to discover the kind of person he or she wishes to marry. Back in the "Happy Days" era, we dated several people before "going steady." I arrived at a girlfriend's house one evening to discover that her afternoon date was just leaving by the back door.

In the life cycle of a congregation, the goal for finding a match is to discover a place or group of people to reach for Christ through starting a church. Several possibilities may surface as a congregation prays for God's direction and seeks to match needs and resources.

Discovery of the need for new congregations may occur in various ways. A Christian whose relative lives in an area without a church may promote the idea of developing a congregation there.

A denomination or prospective sponsoring church may discover the need for a church through a region-wide survey.

Southern Baptists have two survey methods that have proven effective in locating places to plant churches. The Church Starting Probe is used in Anglo- and African-American communities and a Laser Thrust is used in ethnic/language communities.

These methods are used in "associations," groups of churches that work and fellowship together.

Three sets of statistics are used in the Probe.

1) Demographics. The census bureau, the county school board, regional planning office, or the highway commission can supply this

information. Note the growth patterns of the past and projections for the future.

2) Ten-year growth pattern of Southern Baptist churches in the association. Annual minutes of the association are sources for these figures.

3) Information related to other churches in the association. The best source of information is the local churches. The Glenmary Research Center lists church membership in U.S. counties.[1]

For the Probe, the association is divided into two to eight zones, depending on size and population. Teams drive through each zone to survey new-work needs. Each team recommends places to start new work in their zone.

The association prioritizes the list of new-work needs. Churches are then enlisted to sponsor new congregations in those places.

This chapter gives an overview of community types, people groups, and housing patterns as they relate to the need for churches. It also examines traits of people and their effects on new congregations.

Places to Find a Match

It is helpful to look at people in three ways—by geography (location), demographics (numbers), and psychographics (groupings). The first is a geographical look. Where are the people located?

Geography

Location: Growth Communities.—Possibly the most fertile fields for new churches are areas that have experienced significant population growth in the past ten years. Church growth should occur as the population grows. This can happen in two ways—as churches assimilate newcomers and as they start additional churches.

Several years ago a number of new towns sprang up in one state. Developers established planned resort communities where small communities had existed. Out-of-state retirees became residents of the new towns.

When existing churches dealt with an influx of newcomers, they were unable to assimilate large numbers of new people. Older churches accepted only a few new families comfortably. But when 30-40 percent of a congregation were newcomers, trauma resulted. Newcomers did not feel at home in many existing churches because of socioeconomic positions.

In this situation, large numbers of people relocated to the new communities, but established churches grew only slightly. New churches sprang up and experienced tremendous growth, primarily from the newcomers.

Suburbs continue to develop around metropolitan areas. Most urban areas follow a general growth pattern. People move away from the inner-city and other city areas. An interstate-type beltway encircles the area. Eventually, a second beltway develops as the metropolitan area grows.

Church planting thrives in the suburbs, even in economically slow times. More than any other location, the suburbs are home to new, growing congregations.[2]

Some church members who move to outlying areas drive back to their city churches, but most do not. Generally, people will travel no more than twenty minutes to attend church, unless it is a mega church. Participation usually lessens when the church is located at a great distance. Therefore, new suburbs need new churches for relocated church members as well as for the unchurched.

Rural fringe and urban fringe communities often need new churches. In the past, many communities were little country villages. As urban sprawl developed, some outlying villages became thriving rural fringe communities. New people moved from the cities to live in rural areas.

Dailey, West Virginia, is an example. In a twenty-year period, its population quadrupled. The people were not clustered in a town.

Many lived in homes built along rural country roads within a five-mile radius of Dailey.

Most of the rural fringe communities had small country churches, the majority of which were family chapels. Those churches did not grow significantly, even though the population doubled or tripled. As population grows, the best way to include the new people in church is to begin congregations.

The urban fringe community is at the edge of the developing urban area. It is also an area to consider for new churches.

Location: Isolated Neighborhoods. —A community may become isolated because of interstate highway construction. Rivers, railroads, parks, or industrial development are other factors that contribute to separating parts of a community from the whole. In some cases, churches may be needed in these areas.

Location: Changing Communities. —When church members move away from communities experiencing socioeconomic change, churches often relocate. This happens especially in inner cities. Churches may move to the suburbs to follow their congregations. Churches should be available for people who continue to live in inner cities.

Racial change also occurs in communities. One racial group moves away and another becomes predominant in the community. Churches may move away. A new church may be needed for the new group of residents.

Social and economic change often occur as residents leave a community. Communities that were upper middle-class thirty years ago change dramatically as lower-income residents move in. Sometimes churches exist in these communities, but the members no longer live in the neighborhood. Furthermore, the local people do not attend, even though a church may be located near them. A new church is needed to reach new community residents.

As communities change, housing patterns change. As owners

move to other locations, large, expensive homes may be converted into apartments or duplexes.

Usually decreased economic conditions accompany this kind of change. People who occupy the apartments are usually singles or families who have not yet been able to purchase their first homes. Most are renters rather than owners. A new church may be needed to accommodate young families and singles.

Location: Multihousing. — Another way to discover places to plant new churches is to look at housing patterns. Some current housing patterns that divide people from the larger society hinder the church's reaching them. David Bunch, Harvey J. Kneisel, and Barbara L. Oden identify several categories of multihousing—low-rise contained communities, high-rise, inaccessible contained communities, total residential, public housing, manufactured housing, and unperceived multihousing.[3] These multihousing communities cluster residents in identifiable neighborhoods.

Bunch reports that 28 percent, or seventy million U.S. residents now live in multihousing. Many factors divide these people from the larger population. Only about 4 percent of multihousing community residents attend existing churches.

One barrier that prevents churches from reaching people in multihousing is the attitudes of people who live in manufactured housing communities. They see themselves as set apart from the larger community. They are not sure that the schools want their children, that the community wants their mobile home park, or that the churches want them in attendance.

The physical arrangement in multihousing is another barrier. People grouped together in a high-rise or apartment complex may have security guards or entrance gates sheltering the residents. Many communities have "No Solicitation" signs and consider churches to be solicitors. Security guards have stopped summer missionaries and others from knocking on doors in multihousing communities.

Bunch, in his strategies for reaching these people, concludes that "establishing a congregation identified with the multihousing community may be the most effective way to reach residents with the gospel."[4] Those who have attempted to minister to people inside multihousing communities have discovered that owners and most of the residents are receptive to their coming. Some new congregations inside multihousing communities reach up to 30 percent of the residents.

Those who wish to begin new congregations in these communities need to learn how to do so in ways that conform to particular housing patterns of the communities. Bunch's book gives the experiences of people who have started new congregations. Principles and activities they incorporated offer help to other church starters.

Demographics

The second way to locate a place to plant is to consider the demographics. Census information can reveal a great deal about the people of a community.

When preparing to start a church, the sponsoring group should know how many people live in the area. They also need information about age, group divisions, family income levels, housing patterns, family composition and distribution, and educational levels. See appendix A for a sample demographic readout of a Douglas County, Georgia, community.

In appendix A, third paragraph, "Age Distribution," note that 25.5 percent of the people are ages thirty to forty-four. The community composition is predominantly young to middle-aged adults. Seventeen percent of the children are under age nine and 20.9 percent are ages ten to nineteen.

These demographics indicate that a new church should major on families with children and teenagers. A meeting place to accommodate preschool children will be essential. A program and workers for teens will be vital from the start.

Appendix A, second paragraph, "Household Income," notes the majority of the families (60 percent) are in the middle income bracket

($15 to $36 thousand). This indicates that in the future the community will be able to support a church without outside assistance.

Psychographics

A third way to locate a new church site is to identify groups of people in the same vicinity who are "united by a common culture, tradition, or sense of kinship, that typically have common language, institutions, and beliefs" (Webster's definition of *peoples*).

Psychographic information offers the church planter a more personal view of people. It reveals something of their life-styles, values, and aspirations. It shows their felt needs.

Sometimes a people group is a subgroup of a larger segment of society. For example, a German ethnic community in Iowa is a part of Anglo America. But in the cultural aspects of their lives they still hold to many of the values and practices of the German community.

Church planters should be aware of residents' values and life-styles in order to succeed in starting churches in people group communities. Church planters should strive to establish significant relationships within people groups in preparation for successful church planting.

George Barna Research has also discovered some interesting facts about the American family in the 1990s: Only 35 percent have children; the typical family is composed of two working parents and one school-age child; one parent has been divorced; 57 percent of women now work outside the home, and 56 percent of children want a close relationship with God.[5]

New churches should develop programs to relate to family life-styles. If demographics indicate a large senior citizen population, sponsoring-church expectations and plans would differ. Ministries, structure, and programs relating to senior citizens may need strong emphasis.

The business world identifies groups of people with common characteristics in order to sell products. They call this "market segmentation." Christians should know the characteristics of the people they intend to reach. Jesus said His followers are to be "as shrewd as snakes and as innocent as doves" (Matt. 10:16, NIV). One company that sells psychographic information on communities is CACI of Fairfax, Virginia, 1-800-292-2240. Their printout is called ACORN.

Refer to appendix B for a psychographics printout of the Douglas County, Georgia, community for which we had demographics. Three or four basic groups emerge: middle Americans (13.7 percent) and start-up families (42.1 percent) would be comfortable with one another in the same church. Baby boomers (21.7 percent) might also fit with these groups. The minimum wage families (14.4 percent) probably would need their own style of church. Settled families (8.2 percent) would not likely attend the younger family church.

Douglas County is 50 percent unchurched. Combining the numbers of start-up families and middle Americans in new homes gives a total of 7,159 people. Half of that is 3,580 unchurched people. If a church reached 10 percent of that target group, the church potential is 358, a substantial church. If a sponsor chose one of the other groups, it could expect to develop a smaller congregation that may never have a fully supported pastor. However, to reach this Douglas County community, three new churches may be needed.

Lyle Schaller says, "If the goal is to reach younger generations of adults, one of the assets in achieving that goal is to be able to offer people choices."[6]

The Southern Baptist Home Mission Board Research Division provides printouts for new congregations that Southern Baptists sponsor. The printouts include explanations of community groups. See appendix C for a sample.

Among the corporations that provide this kind of service are Claritas Corporation of Alexandria, Virginia, 1-703-683-8300; National Decision Systems of Encinitas, California; and Donnelley Marketing Information Corporation of Stamford, Connecticut, 1-800-866-2255.

Because psychographics indicate something of people's values and life-styles, this valuable planning tool can point to worship and pastoral leadership styles a group might prefer. David Putman points out that even publicity and media use are related to the kind of group from whom church starters wish a positive response.[7]

In their article "Harnessing Old and New Technology in Church Planting," Carol Childress, Gordon Lawrence, and Larry Wartsbaugh look at the implications of psychographic information for church planting. They draw conclusions related to style of church, size, methods of ministry, and decision making.[8]

Other sources also report on the values people hold. George Barna reports that most U.S. residents have no philosophy of life. He says 63 percent hold the purpose of life to be personal enjoyment; 66 percent believe there is no absolute truth; and 52 percent think their first responsibility is to self.[9]

Needs and Interests

Discovering the needs and interests of the group you want to reach is another consideration for "making a match." Everybody has felt needs. In 1980 Rick Warren's church-starting approach in Orange County, California, was to visit large numbers of people and learn of their interests and concerns through an opinion survey. Today, that church, Saddleback Valley Community Church, has a weekly attendance of more than four thousand.

Paul Powell says, "Those churches that are really alive are the ones that are discovering and ministering to people's needs."[10]

Some groups may tend to reject a religious survey. An interest survey may be more appealing. (See appendixes D and E for sample survey forms.) The Christian community may see certain needs among the unchurched, such as counseling or family enrichment. Unchurched people may be unaware of their needs. To be successful in reaching people, church planters need to identify the attitudes and mind-set of those they want to reach. Inspired by the Holy Spirit, Paul wrote, "Though I am free and belong to no man, I make myself a slave to everyone, to win as many as possible. To the weak I became weak, to win the weak. I have become all things to all men so that by all possible means I might save some. I do all this for the sake of the gospel" (1 Cor. 9:19,22-23, NIV).

To receive a good response from a particular group, a church starter's approach should be based on the group's felt needs and interests. "The customer is king" attitude is characteristic of the United States in the 1990s.[11]

With all the information in hand, how does one "make a match"? The sponsoring church should concentrate on discovering what the target community is really like. Sponsoring-church workers who will help launch a new church should be compatible with the people of the community. For example, in targeting young adults, the sponsor would be wise to enlist young adult workers rather than a group of seniors. One or two workers could be in the senior category, but most of the workers should be able to closely identify with and understand the target group.

Project the Future

We can now ask, "How can you project the future by knowing geography, demographics, and psychographics?" Certain questions arise such as: What meeting places are available? Do we need to buy land soon, later, or not at all? What size building will we need? When should we build? People need to have some idea about the potential size of a new church and its ministry style. Figures on current population growth or decline and projections can help answer some questions.

A permanent meeting place is not necessary in the early stages of church starting. However, some sponsoring churches are able to purchase land very early in the process. A sponsoring church or denomination might be able to purchase desirable property at a reasonable price in smaller towns.

How much land should be purchased? A rule of thumb practiced by the Southern Baptist Church Loans Division of the Home Mission

Board and other denominations is that one acre will accommodate one hundred people.

It is unreasonable to expect that any church is going to reach 100 percent of the unchurched population in a given community. The best way to determine the potential percentage a new church might reach is to observe older churches in the same area. A church that is forty years old has probably reached its maximum size. What percentage did it reach? A safe national percentage would be 10 percent. Long-range plans should include these figures.

Obviously, a church in a large metropolitan area would not be able to build a church large enough to accommodate all the unchurched. Therefore, it should consider church starts or satellite ministries in different communities or groupings within the area.

Socioeconomic groupings have a bearing on how large churches will become. For example, people in low-income groups are generally members of churches with attendance of less than one hundred. For church planting in a low-income area, a strategy might be to consider planting several smaller churches. Land purchase, then, would be in keeping with the anticipated size of the churches.

Having complete information about a field or group that needs a new church can assist a potential sponsoring church in the decision to sponsor. Sometimes denominational leaders visit a potential sponsoring church to share the information about needs.

At this point, the Missions Council and the pastor should answer several questions: Is this the type of new start our church could successfully sponsor? Can we provide the needed resources? Should we enlist a partnership sponsor for the project? Do we need assistance from our denomination? Is the timing right? Do we believe God is leading us to proceed?

Like the young adult who has discovered all he needs to know about a marriage prospect, they are ready to take the prospect home to meet the family.

MEETING THE IN-LAWS 4

The Preparation Stage

Mary Ida and I dated for several months before I was invited to spend an evening with her parents. I had heard only good things about her parents and had met them casually. Yet when the night arrived for me to go to their home, I was nervous. *Would we like each other? Would they approve of me?*

Eager to begin the evening, I arrived early. Mary Ida's mother was seated in a chair where she remained the entire evening. Mr. Campbell met me at the door and welcomed me inside. We played table games and I began to feel comfortable with them. The Campbells smiled a lot all evening. Mrs. Campbell never left her chair, so I finally made my departure without time alone with my girlfriend.

After we were married I learned more about that evening. Mrs. Campbell had been resting in a chair, with her work skirt over her lap, before changing to meet me. When I arrived early, she was caught in the chair for the evening. I suspect I was not the only nervous one that evening.

Vital relationships carry a high value. Having time to get accustomed to the idea of a future son-in-law is important. A mother church also needs preparation time in order to build a vital relationship with its mission congregation.

Initial Contact

A first step in sponsorship preparation is for the pastor to become convinced that his church could be even more useful to the Lord by starting a new congregation. Charles Chaney says, "America will not be won to Christ by existing churches, even if they should suddenly become vibrantly and evangelistically alive."[1] The pastor should recognize that sponsorship can be a blessing for the sponsor as well as for the new congregation.

Members of twenty sponsoring churches in the Arkansas Baptist State Convention were asked about their churches' sponsorship of new starts. Some answers were: "I feel that our church is not a self-centered institution." "I like to give to our church because it is sharing to start a new church." "Our church has been more unified since it started sponsoring a new church."

First Baptist Church of Rogers, Arkansas, sponsored Calvary Baptist Chapel in the same city. Sponsoring pastor Ben Rowell said, "We gave some of our best people to work in Calvary Mission. Our church was blessed far beyond what we gave."[2]

Carl F. George of the Charles E. Fuller Institute of Evangelism and Church Growth speaks of "churches that start new missions with a group of people from their church. One year later the mother church will be larger."[3]

Churches that help sponsor new congregations seem to attract new members who desire a high level of involvement. Sponsorship also calls members to greater commitment.

Leadership Group

The second step is for the church to designate a group to handle the mission project, such as a Missions Development Council.

An ideal Missions Development Council would be composed of members respected by the church, but not overloaded with other jobs. They should be capable of understanding data and influencing the congregation. They should favor sponsoring a new congregation.

Designation of a leadership group should signal that something important is taking place. The council should have a representative from each major group in the church, including Sunday School and missions groups.

Denominational materials may be used for training and orientation of the council. This training should cover how to relate to the church, the duties of each council member, and the general steps for starting a new congregation.

After training, the council begins to do its homework. This means determining if all pertinent information is in hand: number of people living in the community, age breakdown, number of unchurched, number who own and rent, marital status, family makeup, income levels, education, and housing patterns. (See appendix F for An Area Analysis form.) This data—except the number of unchurched—can come from the census. The ACORN information may come from a market-segmentation report.

The council may meet with the finance committee to discuss mission financing before making a recommendation to the church. Together, they determine a preliminary budget. (See appendix G for a sample Church Budget Worksheet.)

The target group for the new church governs budget requirements. Low-income church starts need less funding per year. But they will be slower to reach self-support. The average church can support a full-time pastor, a building program, and church ministries when it has about two hundred members. Some missions in small neighborhoods may never become self-supporting in this sense. If the new congregation does not have the potential for supporting a full-time pastor, sponsors should consider a bivocational leader.

A new start in a more affluent area requires larger amounts of money in the first two years. It needs quality ministries to reach the people group. The new work will probably be self-supporting within three years.

Mission Types

The Missions Development Council needs clear agreement on the type of mission congregation needed. I am using *congregation* to mean a group of people with a separate identity who together practice regular worship, Bible study, witness, missions, ministry, and fellowship. The congregation may take several forms.

The first model is the **church-type mission.** A new congregation is formed with the express purpose of becoming a self-sustaining congregation. The sponsors plan to assist the new congregation until it can stand alone.

A second model may be a **permanent mission.** This congregation may never become self-supporting. Ebbie Smith says, "Most denominations are missing great opportunities by not establishing churches among the very poor who may constitute the greatest mission field in the United States."[4] The permanent mission is not expected to constitute as a church. For example, it may meet in a multihousing community with rapid turnover, or it could be a congregation in a retirement home.

Sponsoring churches will expect to continue supplying finances and workers to sustain a permanent mission. The mission will be an ongoing part of the church's outreach.

A third kind of new congregation is the **satellite**—a part of the sponsoring-church congregation that meets in a location apart from the church building. Usually, a satellite conducts a full program of worship, Bible study, evangelism, fellowship, and ministry. The sponsoring-church staff may provide leadership. Some churches have used the satellite approach before moving to a new location. Some churches use the term *satellite* to denote almost any kind of mission congregation that meets away from the sponsoring church. A satellite congregation may or may not become a constituted church.

The **mission Sunday School** is a fourth approach to mission outreach. This mission method works well where children are the primary group involved. The sponsor should provide a Sunday School class for every age group. Temporary mission Sunday Schools are sometimes planned for migrant laborers during summer months. In some cases, a mission Sunday School may develop into a church-type mission.

A fifth mission type is the **sister-church** approach. This mission method is effective when a mission group needs financial assistance, workers, and guidance. An established church may form a sister relationship with the congregation to help it grow. This kind of partnership can benefit both groups. In the beginning, the groups involved should formulate an agreement regarding the expectations and functions of each group.

A sixth mission approach is the **house church.** New Testament church groups met in homes. Paul sent greetings to Priscilla and Aquila and "the church that meets at their house" (Rom. 16:5, NIV). After Pentecost, the believers "broke bread in their homes and ate together with glad and sincere hearts, praising God and enjoying the favor of all the people. And the Lord added to their number daily those who were being saved" (Acts 2:46-47, NIV). Paul and Silas "spoke the word of the Lord to him [Philippian jailer] and to all the others in his house" (16:32, NIV).

What is a house church? It is a congregation meeting in a dwelling to conduct regular worship, study the Bible, and have fellowship. Members witness and practice missions. It has its own identity as a congregation.

The house church approach has several strengths: 1) It meets some people's desire for a small church. 2) It is "cost effective" for the sponsoring church. 3) It is flexible. For example, it may change the meeting place to another house with minimum effort. 4) It usually meets in a densely populated neighborhood. Transportation is not required to get to church. 5) It is usually composed of one or two homogenous groups. The people are comfortable with one another. 6) New house churches can be formed quickly.

Conversely, the house church approach has weaknesses: 1) Urban areas may view a house church as a violation of zoning and safety codes. 2) Some people hesitate to attend church in a home. 3) Worship and teaching materials must usually be carried in and out each week. 4) Ministry activities may be limited. 5) Growth potential is limited.

What happens to house churches? The majority move to more permanent locations. Some change locations. Others discontinue.

Ebbie Smith says, "Evangelizing and congregationalizing this world demands a diversity of types of churches."[5] Before making a recommendation to the church, the Missions Development Council should determine the type of mission needed. Unrealistic expectations for the type of mission established can result in disappointment.

Sponsorship Approaches

Another decision to be determined by the council is the type of sponsor the church might become. Several sponsorship approaches may be effective.

(1) *Primary sponsor.*—More than one established congregation may help start and develop a new congregation. In this case, one church should serve as the primary sponsor. The primary sponsor holds the membership records of the new group and makes final decisions about procedures in beginning the congregation.

If several sponsoring congregations are located in the same area, committee members representing the churches can relate to the primary sponsor.

(2) *Cosponsor.*—A cosponsoring church provides financial assistance and perhaps workers. The primary sponsor still makes final decisions.

(3) *Support or associate sponsor.*—This type sponsor provides a stated amount of financial support, prays for the new work, and may send workers for special projects.

(4) *Sponsoring church and denomination.*—The denomination may assist the sponsoring church in providing financial support and counsel needed by the new church. The sponsoring church manages the mission.

I concur with Charles Chaney, "Church planting . . . is those things one existing Christian fellowship does to share its faith in Jesus Christ with another community of people and to form them into a new congregation of responsible disciples of Jesus Christ."[6] The church is the basic biblical unit. Where, then, do denominational districts, associations, conferences, state conventions, and national bodies fit? A group of churches may accomplish more than one church can do alone.

Several church-planting functions may be performed by a religious organization related to local churches without usurping the role of the local church. Some of these functions are:

- Encourage a positive church-planting climate.
- Identify places and people groups needing new churches.
- Generate prayer support from a wide group of churches.
- Provide networking for church planters to share ideas and methods with one another.
- Recruit and deploy church-planter missionaries to places where local churches are too few or too weak to start churches.
- Provide training and materials for planting new churches.

(5) *Sponsor.* —Some churches are strong enough to start and develop a new congregation without outside help. First Baptist Church of Arlington, Texas, sponsors more than one hundred satellite missions.

The Missions Development Council needs full information about the target group or community, a preliminary budget proposal, and agreement as to the type of mission needed. The council should be prepared to explain to the church the type of sponsor relationship the church will have with the mission.

Church members will have questions. A wise council will prepare to answer questions before making a recommendation. The following questions are often heard: Why can't the community's existing churches reach the people? How many people need to be reached? What are the people like who live in the target community? How long will our church need to be involved? How much will it cost?

The Decision to Sponsor

Several examples in the Book of Acts give us models for concerned and involved sponsors.

The Jerusalem church sent Peter and John to Samaria where people had responded to Philip's preaching (see Acts 8:14). Acts 11:22 records that the Jerusalem church received news that people were turning to the Lord and sent Barnabas to Antioch.

The decision to sponsor should be a spiritual highlight for a church. The Missions Development Council and pastor should request and lead informed prayer times before the decision. The church attitude should be, "This is God's business. We want His leadership. We want to follow His will each step of the way."

My observations about sponsors indicate that the following process can help a church practice informed praying and have a positive spiritual experience in sponsorship.

(1) The pastor should lead the way by preaching on missions or inviting a church-starting specialist to preach. In any case, the church should know the pastor is in favor of the project. Scriptural bases for messages are: Matthew 28:18-20; Acts 1:8; 11:19-26; 16:9-40; and many others.

(2) Bible study groups may plan a church-planting study. Church members need to see that church planting is biblical, not just another program.

(3) Share the mission field information with all major groups of the church. This should include men's and women's groups, deacons, and others.

Serious objections or questions should be noted. The council should prepare an answer for each.

(4) Share information about the opportunity of sponsorship in a variety of ways. Hearing a testimony from someone in the target community or group can boost enthusiasm for a new start.

Use the church newsletter and handouts to worshipers to share information about the opportunities of sponsorship.

(5) Again, I emphasize that the whole process should be bathed in prayer. The congregation not only needs information about the need, but it should seek the Lord's will about being involved. Is this God's time? The congregation should decide that God is leading in the process before proceeding.

Include prayer times for a proposed new church start in worship services, midweek prayer services, Sunday School classes, group meetings, and family worship.

After the church is fully prepared to make a godly decision, the Missions Development Council should present a recommendation to the church for official action.

The council may develop a recommendation something like this: "The Missions Development Council, after thorough research, fervent prayer, and much discussion with church groups, recommends that _____ Church sponsor a new congregation in the _____ community.

After the Decision to Sponsor

When the church decides to sponsor, the decision should be widely publicized through worship announcements, the church newsletter, and in other ways.

The Missions Development Council should develop a growth plan. This plan should include calling a pastor, growth goals, meeting places, workers, financing, launch date, land and buildings, and constitutional plans. (See appendix H for a sample Church Starting Planning Form.)

A preliminary budget may be recommended in relation to the kind of mission start the church approves. Major budget items will be pastoral support, outreach, meeting place, and ministries.

At this point, challenge members to become involved in the mission project. God has gifted and will inspire some people to work in the new start. Some may work for six months to one year. Others may become permanent members of the new congregation.

People from the sponsoring church who become a part of the mission should be compatible with the unchurched people the mission intends to reach. Incompatibility can result in slow growth or no growth.

The pastor and Missions Development Council may prayerfully consider which individuals might be most effective in the mission congregation, then approach them about service. (See appendix I for considerations in choosing a mission fellowship leader.) The group of workers and the mission leader will spell success or failure for the new work. Church members who live in the new-work community may be likely workers. They should be elected by the church.

A commissioning service for workers in the mission can be a meaningful experience for the church and the workers. (See appendix J for a Sample Commissioning Service.) A dedication prayer will remind workers of the church's prayer support. A commissioning service affirms the new work and the workers.

It would be ideal for the sponsoring church to call a mission pastor at this point. (See chapter 7 for a discussion of pastoral characteristics.)

All of this may seem like a lot of preparation. But any relationship improves with understanding and communication. I still enjoy table games with my in-laws. We now laugh together about embarrassing situations of the past.

The Missionary Phase

Church planting as recorded in the Book of Acts had a missionary phase and a church phase. In the missionary phase, the church at Antioch, led by the Spirit, sent Paul and Barnabas on their first missionary journey (see Acts 13:2-4). The missionaries traveled to places of regional influence such as Salamis, Pisidian Antioch, and Iconium.

The missionary teams described in Acts preached, taught, built relationships, identified leaders, and witnessed to individuals and groups. They also suffered persecution and hardship, revealed the power of God, and gathered believers to establish churches.

Some American locations need the missionary phase of church

planting. Conditions dictate that some works need to be missionary centered. When a sponsoring church is more than fifty miles away, it is impractical to send workers on a regular basis to assist a new work. The denomination may not have a local congregation.

Several denominational groups have a goal of establishing at least one congregation in every county in the United States. Much of this church planting will be in the missionary phase.

Selection of missionaries is the key to success in the missionary phase. The leadership of the Holy Spirit is essential. Under His leadership, the sponsoring group carefully selects missionaries whom they feel are called of God, dedicated to Christ, and solid in the faith. The sending group should be convinced that the missionaries are capable of planting a church. Missionaries in Acts generally worked in teams. The missionary family is the most common team in our day.

Missionaries need support from the sending group. Occasional visits to the missionary field are encouraging. Communication and assurance of prayer support are vital.

The missionary should communicate continually with the sending group, keeping them fully informed about needs, progress, victories, and hardships. Sometimes the sending group needs involvement in decision making. In all cases, the missionary should work to have a base of prayer support and saturate all he does in prayer.

The specific approach the missionary uses to start the new work will depend on his spiritual gifts and strengths. Missionaries have used the process described below for several hundred successful starts.

The missionary finds a specific community or people group that needs a church. He seeks and finds God's purpose for him related to starting a church in that place. Then the sending group commissions him as a fully funded church planter, a bivocational minister, or Christian volunteer.

The missionary ministers on the target field the following ways:

(1) Becomes familiar with available data such as psychographics (ACORN) and demographics. From the data, learns the population of

the area, the number of unchurched, and characteristics, values, and life-styles of the people.

(2) Visits and builds relationships with community leaders such as school administrators, postal workers, mayor, sheriff, other public officials, religious leaders, and human resource personnel. Learns about their work and the community. By inquiring about community needs, conveys intention to be a positive force for good.

(3) Visits at least one hundred community families to identify felt needs in the community.

(4) Chooses one or two ministries related to the needs and concerns of the people. Uses spiritual gifts, personality strengths, and other resources to minister effectively.

(5) Discovers one to three families that will host Bible studies in their homes. Develops the mission fellowship from which the core group of workers must come.

(6) May conduct a telephone or house-to-house survey to build a list of unchurched people in the area.

(7) Prepares the mission fellowship group(s) to launch a new congregation (See chapters 7 and 8).

(8) Becomes pastor of the mission.

(9) Involves the core group in everything they can do in the new mission congregation. Begins to spend more time equipping and involving members in the work of ministry.

(10) Continues to witness to individuals, develop disciples, and lead the group toward maturity (See Eph. 4:11-16).

(11) When the mission becomes biblically sound and has sufficient workers to carry on the functions of a church and enough financial strength to sustain itself, the missionary leads in constituting the mission into a church.

(12) At this point, the missionary must decide if he is called to continue as the pastor of this congregation or to begin again in another place.

After the missionaries in Acts planted churches in the major population centers, they traveled to other locations. In the second phase of church planting, local congregations continued to plant churches in their areas.

Both phases of church planting are needed in the United States today. Some major areas need scores of new churches. The San Francisco Bay Area, for instance, has 5.5 million people, 85 percent of whom are unchurched. In the Los Angeles area, 80 percent of the 4.5 million people are unchurched. Denominational organizations should saturate such areas with missionaries like Priscilla, Aquila, Titus, and Timothy. Once churches have been established, the "church phase" can be effective in evangelizing the population.

THE
5 ENGAGEMENT

The Cultivation Stage

Mike prepared his marriage proposal carefully. To convince Stephanie of his undying love, he said, "I would run the Boston marathon if you were the trophy. I would race in the Indianapolis 500 to win your love. I would ride a space shuttle to the moon if you lived there. If I had a thousand arms, I would love you with every one."

Stephanie was not in the mood for speeches. She interrupted to say, "Stop your lying, Mike. You're not even using the two good arms you have."

In the engagement period (cultivation stage), a sponsor must convince the community or target group of its sincerity and intentions to start a permanent church. The goal is to raise the community's awareness of the new congregation. The sponsor will seek to perform a genuine ministry and relate to the community in such a way that the ministry earns the respect of the people in the target community.

Who leads the cultivation activities? If the sponsoring church is near, it should carry out the actions. If a mission pastor has been designated, he will lead the cultivation activities. It earns goodwill for the church planter to be identified with community ministries. If a pastor has not yet been chosen, the Missions Development Council should lead community events and ministries.

Love Is Spelled S-E-R-V-I-C-E

Mike had the right idea in expressing his love by telling what he was willing to do for Stephanie. A first step in cultivating the new community is to find some felt needs and meet them in the name of Christ. Select one or two needs and do an excellent job of meeting them. Do an attitude check—Is the ministry done with genuine concern for the people?

One of the best ways to discover community needs is to ask local people. The inquiry indicates your interest in the people. This heightens community interest and acceptance. It is good practice for a church-planter pastor to visit at least one hundred families his first month on the field. This shows his interest in the people and gives him the "feel" of the community.

One opinion survey includes this question, "What do you think are the greatest needs of the people in this community?" The question is raised in a nonthreatening, impersonal manner. Answers reflect the personal feelings of the people. (See appendixes D and E for survey forms.)

Many people in a newly developed community where a church was beginning said, "We need a place to get together for recreation and body building."

The church determined that their first unit needed to be a multipurpose building for community recreation. Even in their rented facility, this new congregation offered exercise classes that proved to be a very successful connection and ministry in the community.

Many other ministries may be initiated during the cultivation stage. Visiting homebound people has proven successful. This ministry does not cost anything. Visitors can share Christian literature, taped worship services, Bible studies, and Christian music. The main purpose is to express Christian concern through visits with homebound people.

Other possible ministries include services for the handicapped, volunteer chaplaincy programs, nursing home visits, transportation for the elderly, Mother's Day Out, recreation for youth, and food and clothing closets.

At this point, observe a warning flag related to ministry. Engaging in a ministry does not ensure the growth and progress of a new congregation. Many of the people to whom the new church may minister will never come to the church. Some of them may not be physically able to attend. Others may feel embarrassed that they receive food or clothing help. Recipients may attend church, but it may not be the one that ministered to them.

Jack Redford, former Church Extension director, Home Mission Board, SBC, tells of two churches. One "grew because the ministries reached into the community, building bridges. The ministries were the springboard to witness, and witness to professions of faith. The ministries were part of the church, expanding into evangelism and outreach. One grew and one failed because one maintained a redemptive note, and the other forgot why it was on the bridge."[1]

Affluent people may not respond well to questions about their "needs." Yet they have "interests and concerns." The church may join with them in family enrichment seminars or self-enhancement conferences.

Many times ministry opens the door for evangelistic witnessing—to those served and to people who respect the church because of its ministry. Ministry authenticates the church's right to witness. We earn the right to share the good news of the gospel with those who do not have it.

Individual Christians and the church body minister because of their nature. Jesus said, "Whatever you did for one of the least of these brothers of mine, you did for me" (Matt. 25:40, NIV).

Ministry in church planting is a vital issue. Ministry should be done in the community even before the church is started. This not only earns respect for the new congregation, but it expresses what the church is going to be in that community.

Community Events

Engaged couples go places together. It helps them to better understand one another and become closer friends. Planned community events should be part of cultivation. They help make friends and build understanding.

Community events may include puppet shows; musicals in the downtown square, shopping center, or mall; mission Vacation Bible Schools; Backyard Bible Clubs; craft classes; revivals; dramas; parenting and self-improvement seminars; picnics; and even surveys. Mike Hoffman, a church starter in the Georgia Baptist Convention, sponsored a money management seminar for young adults in an apartment complex.

A sponsoring church can increase its potential by inviting other groups of its denomination to assist with community events. People from other communities or distant areas may be available to help.

Records of cultivative events should include names, addresses, and phone numbers of those who attend. The information becomes an excellent mailing list when the new church is launched.

Meeting and visiting community leaders is a rewarding cultivative action. These might include the mayor, Chamber of Commerce president, school superintendent, county sheriff, county extension agent, home economist, newspaper editor or owner, and TV and radio station managers.

As these people learn of your concerns and interests in the community, they can share their views about services a church could provide.

An excellent cultivation activity is building relationships with existing community churches. Seek out the president of the ministerial association. Let this person and other pastors know that the new church will be there to reach the unchurched, not to enlist their members. You may have opportunity to join with other churches in a community project.

Publicity is crucial to any community event. A general tract, brochure, or flier advertising special events may be mailed to all residents. Free publicity may be available through radio, TV, and newspapers. The cultivation team should take advantage of those opportunities. The most attractive publicity comes when people like what is going on and excitedly share this with neighbors and friends.

Open Doors

A young person with selfless love for a fiance looks for opportunities to be available in times of need. A sponsoring church should watch for open doors for service in the new community it is courting.

A company transfer of new people into a community and the addition of new housing are open doors. Church members may visit these people and provide a welcome service.

A church moving out of an inner-city area may open a door because of the spiritual vacuum left in the community. A new church may start relating to the people left in the community who are not moving with the old church.

Another open door may be subdivision lots designated for churches.

Setting a Date

How long is long enough for the engagement period? One indication is that enough ministry has been done to show that the new work can continue successfully without support from the sponsoring group.

A second hallmark of completion of this stage comes when the community is fully aware that the new church is in the making. A third indicator will be that there have been enough community events to provide actual contact and participation with a representative group of the community.

A final indication of a successful engagement period is that the new church has settled many issues about its future. During the cultivation stage, the church should decide about meeting places, leadership, and a beginning date.

Out of community events, workers may have found a home or homes where future Bible studies may be held. If the area where the church is going to be started has several neighborhoods, the cultivation team may want to begin two to six mission fellowships, one in each of the major neighborhoods of the community.

Leadership selection is the most important part of preparation for the "Better or Worse" step coming next. A leader or leaders may come from the sponsoring church or the target field.

Experience indicates that lay people make better fellowship leaders than do preachers. Discussion and participation are important in the fellowship group. People tend to see a preacher as an authority figure. They may be more willing to express their opinions if a lay person is leader.

Leaders should be of unquestionable Christian character. They need a strong biblical faith and a good knowledge of the Scriptures. They should be willing to cooperate with the sponsoring church and those who are leading the church-planting effort.

A date to start a mission fellowship(s) should be set well in advance. Host families need time to invite friends and neighbors to the Bible studies. Some general publicity should go out to inform the community of what is happening. The best way to foster attendance is by a personal invitation from someone already in the group.

When a congregation begins in an area where its denomination is already known and accepted, the cultivation stage may last only a couple of months. If the church seeks to penetrate a new people group or area, cultivation may take up to six months.

The sponsor that has successfully covered the cultivation stage is ready to be joined to the community.

6 FOR BETTER OR WORSE

The Fellowship Stage

My bride and I stood before the preacher at our wedding ceremony with the usual combination of joy and nervousness. I had planned ahead and felt no concern about our car. My good friend, the associational director of missions, lived across the street from the church and had helped me hide the car in his garage. However, I knew we were in trouble when a groomsman came through the line to kiss my bride with a paintbrush sticking out of his back pocket. After the reception, we raced through a shower of rice to the best man's car. Soon most other cars dropped out of pursuit, and we drove to the garage where my car was supposedly "hidden." We made stops at three service stations before we found someone who would wash our well-decorated car.

The fellowship stage deals with the plans and procedures for beginning a mission fellowship. The marriage between a sponsoring group and the community takes place in this stage, "for better or for worse." Plans help make it "for better."

The goal of the fellowship stage is to gather a group of people from the community in which the church will be located. The group must become committed to Christ, to one another, and to beginning a church in their community.

The Mission Fellowship

The mission fellowship is effective for several reasons. 1) It involves and develops a group of people inside the community where the new church will begin. Generating community ownership reduces the risk of future failure. 2) No funds are required to start the group. 3) Workers for the mission generally come from the fellowship group. 4) The fellowship group participates in growth toward the mission stage. 5) The fellowship stage provides time for maturation toward becoming a church. 6) If a mission fellowship dies, the sponsoring group does not have the stigma of a church failure. 7) The fellowship period provides a test of community responsiveness.[1]

The mission fellowship group is not primarily an inward-growth group. It is concerned with outreach to its community. This core group of people will lead and be the heart of a new congregation. Because they live in the community, they will feel ownership of their church as it grows. An outside group could not experience this same sense of ownership.

Plans

The following list includes details that should be planned before the mission fellowship begins.

The location. —The group could meet in a motel or bank meeting room. In many communities the best meeting place is a home or alternate between several homes. Host families should be accepted members of the community. For centuries, new churches have started and met in homes.

Space. —The house or other meeting location needs enough parking space for five or six cars. There should be enough meeting space in the house for children and youth as well as adults.

Size. —A fellowship group is usually small. In fact, when it gets as large as eighteen people, it is time to form another group. At least three families are needed to begin the mission fellowship.

Leadership. —A mission fellowship leader and associate leader should be designated. Both should be present for each meeting. Because a leader does not have time to give attention to everything, the associate may assist. The associate should prepare to lead when the primary leader is absent.

Both the leader and the associate should be grounded in their faith and have a good knowledge of the Scriptures. They should know what they believe and why.

Before the first meeting, leaders should set strong objectives for the group. They should also be trained to some degree in group dynamics and how to lead cell groups. Most of their training may come on the job. Many denominations provide training material related to small groups. A good reference is *Small Group Leaders Handbook*.[2]

Choose leaders worthy of the confidence of the sponsoring-church members. Leaders also should be strongly committed to the idea of a new church in this community.

The church planter who enters a community alone to start a church could begin by leading a Bible study group or groups. If the leader is married, the spouse may serve as associate Bible study leader. Each week, one Bible study group could meet in the daytime and others meet on different nights in the evenings. One Bible study group may be adequate if the community or target group is small.

Publicity. —Choose a group name that will appeal to the community. It could be something like Friendship Community Gathering or Bible Fellowship Meeting.

Two to four weeks before the first meeting, the church planter could prepare a mail-out to all of the people in the area surrounding the fellowship meeting location. Newspapers, TV, and radio could carry the information. Caution may be necessary in some areas because of zoning codes or unsympathetic neighbors.

Word-of-mouth publicity works best. The host family may invite their friends, neighbors, and relatives to come to the meeting. Other families who are going to be involved should invite their contacts.

Approaches. —Two formats function effectively for mission fellowship groups. One approach—the Bible study/discussion format works well with people who are comfortable taking part in group discussions. A second approach—the preaching point—works well with people who feel shy about speaking publicly.

In the Bible study approach, the group (or its leaders) select materials to guide the study. Some groups choose to use only the Bible. Others use Sunday School material. Undated Bible lessons may be used. Commentaries on the Bible may also be a source of study material. Several publishers produce material for Bible study groups.

Whatever the source, the material should be theologically simple. It should use non-church words. The target group is the unchurched people in the area. The people may have little or no church background. Bible study should apply to everyday life but should be Bibie centered.

Some groups may not respond best to a Bible study/discussion group. Participants may fear being asked to read or discuss something publicly. This may discourage some from attending. A better approach for gathering a group in this case may be a preaching point. Few people feel threatened by a worship service. The actual worship service should be limited to no more than one hour.

Young adults who especially like music may also respond better to a preaching point. A worship service including their preferred type of music may attract them better than a Bible study/discussion group.

A home may not be the best place in which to begin a preaching point. It may be better to use a rented room or small community facility. Do not use a large hall where a few people will feel defeated by the size.

Procedures

Whether the Bible study format or preaching point approach is chosen, the mission fellowship will get off to a better start if certain details receive attention. The leader should be present about thirty minutes before the group meets. The host family and leader then greet people as they arrive.

The study should begin on time. The whole session should not be longer than one hour. Your agenda may vary, but include the following.

Begin with some process of getting acquainted. Use name tags. Invite people to introduce and share something about themselves. After the first meeting, greet guests and allow time for all to share life happenings if they wish.

Conduct a prayer time in which you pray for one another and other requests. Avoid too much talk. Above all, avoid gossip. Move quickly into prayer.

After the Bible study session or worship service allow plenty of time for group fellowship. As people visit, they become acquainted and begin to form a solid group. Refreshments are optional. The times before and after the gathering are important if a fellowship group is to jell.

Mission Fellowship Activities

The leader(s) at this point should perform several activities in order to direct the group toward desired goals. One action could be the continuation of ministries begun during the cultivation stage of the new congregation. Those who have been doing the ministry may continue to lead so the community will realize it is a part of the new group's activity.

After its beginning, the Bible study or preaching point should meet consistently. One objective of a new congregation is to gain stability in the new community. Missing a week could have a negative influence on the group's growth.

Another activity is visitation in the homes of those who attend. The leader(s) needs to be prepared to deal with spiritual problems, answer questions about beliefs, and witness to the people regarding their faith in Christ.

The leader(s) should begin to move the Bible study or worship service toward developing an understanding of the nature, purpose, mission, and organization of a church. This is not the time for random discussions. It is the time to move toward the goal of establishing a new congregation.

The mission fellowship should continue for at least two months, but probably no longer than eighteen months. If this group continues together too long without growth or division, it may crystallize into a group in which growth is difficult.

Peter Wagner speaks of building the spiritual dynamic in the following progression:

1. Love—First, we must love one another.
2. Faith—Let them know they are doing something great for God.
3. Prayer—Maintain a consistent life of prayer.
4. Purpose—The objective is to start a new church.[3]

The fellowship stage is usually a one-celled group. Several of these cell groups may meet in the same community. If this is true, they need to come together into a multicelled core group when the cycle moves into the mission stage. Presumably, the different fellowship groups are of the same socioeconomic, language, or ethnic/culture groups. Their original purpose was to form a homogenous unit or core group for a new congregation.

Some adjustments will be necessary when the cell groups come together. A pastor should coordinate and provide leadership for the whole core group. Leaders of the individual cell groups need to become workers in the core group in the uncoming stage.

The mission fellowship is the start-up phase in organizational stages. Among the characteristics of a start-up group are intimate fellowship and a high trust level as described in chapter 1.

A one-cell group consists of up to eighteen people. If several cells are coming together, the group could have as many as fifty or sixty people. A group as large as fifty people has a much better survival rate as a new church than a smaller group. The financial strength of the larger group may prevent difficulties often encountered by a smaller group. A larger number of leaders in a group of more than fifty people adds strength for the work and development of a congregation.

A group of fifty has already broken out of the one-cell group mode. Overcoming that barrier makes growth much easier.

Many successful new congregations began with fewer than fifty people. However, statistics show that the smaller group runs a greater risk of failure.

> In a study of 1,181 Southern Baptist churches organized between 1972 and 1982 . . . 93 of the churches began with 150 or more members. Not one of these churches failed within five years. On the other hand, of the 196 that began with fewer than 25 members, 25 percent were unreported in five years. Churches that begin big have a greater survival rate.[4]

Indications for Launch

How can you know when it is time to move from a mission fellowship stage to an organized mission or chapel? One indicator is that the people in the group are committed to Christ. During the mission fellowship stage, some of them may have become Christians. Others may have experienced a renewal and maturity of faith. Christian growth and excitement about the Lord's work are evident.

Commitment to each other and the group is a second indicator. Members experience intimate fellowship and show concern for others' well-being. Members are also committed to being together as a congregational group.

Third, the group begins to discuss the need for worship and regular Bible study in their community. They are concerned for neighbors and friends who are not in a church. This usually leads to a desire to form a new congregation.

Along with concern, the group has developed an understanding about what a church is and does. The group becomes committed to becoming a part of a New Testament fellowship of believers in their community.

The willingness of individuals to be involved and their commitment to support and work in a new congregation indicate that it is time to move to another stage in the life cycle. Developments needed in preparation for forming a church-type mission congregation are discussed in chapter 7.

THE BLESSED EVENT

7

The Mission Stage

We lived seventy-five minutes from the hospital when we were expecting our first child. Babies, we learned, do not come according to church calendars. The baby was well overdue, and we were into our first Vacation Bible School. Mary, not wanting to sound a false alarm or keep me from Bible School, did not tell me about the contractions before I left.

About midmorning a child interrupted me to say, "Mrs. Tidsworth said you need to come home." In the middle of a sentence, I went home!

After a hurried thirty-minute trip to the doctor's office, we discovered we wouldn't be making the trip to the hospital. Connie was born forty-five minutes later at the doctor's office. Baby and mother were fine. Father? well . . . .

The birth of a mission is a joyous and exciting event. It is indeed a "blessed event." Unexpected things often happen. Much preparation, planning, and prayer precede the event.

Several types of missions—church type mission, permanent mission, satellite, mission Sunday School, and sister church—are discussed in chapter 4.

This chapter deals with the church-type mission. The goal for a church-type mission is to develop a mission fellowship that ultimately becomes a self-supporting congregation. As the congregation reaches people, it grows in leadership and stewardship to the point of being a healthy congregation that functions independently. (See appendix K for a Sample Relationship Agreement between the sponsor and the mission congregation.)

The Church-Planting Pastor

In recent years, discussions have centered on the church-planter or new-work pastor. Researchers and new-work strategists have developed church-planter profiles. Most agree on several basic characteristics of a good church planter.

Church-planting pastors may be divided into at least three categories. First, the **church starter** pulls together the initial core group. The church starter lays the foundation for the new congregation. This beginning leader may be a full-time church-planter missionary who starts core groups and moves on to other communities to repeat the process. Or the person may be a denominational leader, a bivocational church planter, a businessman, or other layperson. The church starter fills a temporary role. Paul was this type of worker.

The second stage leader is the **founding pastor.** In some cases, the church starter may stay with a congregation and become the founding pastor. The founding pastor builds long-term relationships. He concentrates on evangelism and discipleship growth. He organizes the group.

The third stage of pastoral leader is the **growth pastor,** who gives an organized congregation the leadership it needs to grow. He builds on the foundation laid by the church starter and founding pastor. He may lead the church to expand in membership, buildings, ministries, and church planting. At this point, the congregation has the greatest opportunity for numerical growth.

The Church Starter

Bob Logan, vice-president for new church development, Church Resource Ministries (CRM) in Fullerton, California, identifies some essential qualities and skills of a church starter. Logan suggests that a church planter:

- Exercises faith. Exhibits hope, expectation.
- Has vision capacity. Projects into the future. Approaches obstacles as opportunities.
- Is committed to church growth.
- Is personally motivated. Has a desire to do well and a commitment to excellence. Stays with the job. Self-starter. Willing to work hard and long.
- Is responsive to the community. Adapts the church to the character of the community. Doesn't decide what the church will offer before knowing community needs. Disarms the unchurched. (People don't want pressure to attend, give, and do.)
- Creates ownership of ministry. Helps the people feel responsible for growth and development of the church.
- Utilizes people's gifts. Matches people's gifts with tasks to be done.
- Builds cohesiveness.
- Has spouse's cooperation. They share the ministry vision; agree as to each partner's role in the ministry; plan and protect family time by agreeing on guidelines related to home and children; and have a strong family life.
- Is flexible/adaptable. Copes with ambiguity and constant and abrupt change. Adapts methods to current situation.[1]

The Founding Pastor

As a result of my research study of pastors of forty-four young, growing churches, I suggest that the founding pastor:

- Is matched to the local community where a new congregation is beginning.
- Is experienced in the pastorate.
- Is prepared for the field by experience and training.

- Is willing to do most of the work in the beginning stages, but later shares ministry responsibilities.
- Is flexible.
- Has faith and is optimistic.
- Is urgent about progress and patient.
- Is stable enough to stay until results are evident. Knows the costs involved.
- Is enthusiastic about the new church and has a vision for the future.
- Is a strong leader and organizer.
- Is cooperative with the wider fellowship of faith.
- Gives priority to the local field.
- Is a self-starter.
- Is willing to discard ineffective methods and try others.
- Grows personally and professionally.
- Is able to handle criticism and pressure.
- Identifies with the community or group he wants to reach.
- Has a growth attitude.
- Is a good manager of time and works hard.
- Is willing to involve, train, and try lay people as the work grows.
- Preaches and teaches from a biblical base.
- Manages money well.
- Builds good relationships.
- Has a love for God and people.
- Is evangelistic locally. Has a world vision for sharing the gospel.

The Growth Pastor

Characteristics listed for the founding pastor apply to the growth pastor. Other abilities include the following:

- Can keep an organization going.

- Leads in membership growth.
- Is an outstanding preacher.
- Relates well to the larger community.
- Understands church financing.
- Enlarges ministries of the church.
- Can manage and supervise a paid staff.
- May lead in building expansion.

For each type of pastor, we presuppose dedication to Christ, commitment of life to Christ and ministry, and other generally held essentials. But some traits must stand out in the mission pastor. He must be a self-starter. No one will be there to hold his hand. Regular staff meetings are unlikely in a new congregation. Few people will hold him accountable for his day-to-day schedule.

He needs to be a strong leader, sharing vision and focusing direction. On the other side of the coin, he needs to be flexible in method. He should be able to try different approaches and lay them aside if they are not effective. He should be able to adapt to the people with whom he is starting the new church. Those adaptations have to do with methods and approaches, such as worship times and music styles.

Another characteristic that is important is the gift of faith. The mission pastor must be able to see the realities of today, but also recognize the possibilities for tomorrow. What can this church become? He should assess this potential as he looks at the population and the community environment. His vision for the future should say, "This can become reality in this community and for this church."

Match Pastor and Community Profiles

A sponsoring church should try to match the pastor with the community. Demographic and psychographic profiles are discussed in chapter 3. The Missions Development Council should obtain profiles on prospective pastors. Age, educational level, background, life-style, values, and behavior patterns should generally line up with those of the community.

Below is an example of a matched profile.

Community Group	*Pastor*
Start-up families in the twenty-five to thirty-four age group; $15-$35,000 income; majority are college graduates with children.	Seminary graduate, age thirty to thirty-seven, who has served on staff of a growing church; married with one child.

Other considerations in the profile would be leadership style, theological stance, life-style attitude—professional or working-class, preaching style, and general characteristics such as enthusiasm, flexibility, faith, and upward mobility.

Two personality tests can help a potential church planter understand where and how he can best function. (See appendix L for descriptions of The Myers-Briggs Type Indicator and The California Psychological Inventory (CPI).)

Of course, the task of matching community and pastor should be saturated with prayer. The objective is to find God's undershepherd for a community where a new congregation will develop.

Another important aspect of calling a minister is response from the people who will work with him in the new church. Do they believe this is the right person? For example, the mission fellowship group should have the privilege of meeting the pastoral candidate, interviewing, and hearing a sermon. The sponsoring church should give this group opportunity to have a strong voice in the decision to call a pastor. They should be able to anticipate the response that may come from persons in the larger community. The relationship between the pastor and the community is very important to the development of a new congregation.

The mission pastor can be the most important factor in the success or failure of a new congregation. He is the first key to church growth.

People will see him first and will be likely to judge the new congregation by the pastor. Other than the Lord's leadership, nothing is more important than the pastor of a new congregation.

The organizational development of the mission also relates to the type of pastor needed. Some pastors are able to move smoothly through the stages of development. Others serve well in one stage and need to move on to another place when the congregation passes that particular stage.

The sociological level of the mission organization should be considered when determining the type of mission pastor that is needed. (See appendix M for Specialized Functions of Catalyzers, Organizers, and Operators.)

Sociologists identify three levels in human organizations—start-up, organizational, and growth. The type of leadership needed for each stage is described below. A pastor considering a call to a particular mission should determine the mission's stage of development and decide whether he can or desires to work in that stage.

Carl George says the pastor who works with a congregation during the **start-up stage** should be a "catalyzer."[2] A successful start-up pastor usually has an outgoing personality. He is definitely a self-starter. He has a strong vision from the Lord about starting a new church and is a strong leader. He has the gift of faith.

On the other hand, he probably is fairly unorganized and unstructured. He is more like a salesman than an administrator. He may be a little short on patience. He wants to get on with the job.

Second is the **organizational level.** At this level a mission pastor needs organizational skills to help pull things together in the new congregation. A new congregation needs structure and organization. Communication becomes more formal. Policies and procedures for forming additional ministry units should be identified and written down.

The third level in organizational development is the **growth stage.** The pastor leads the church to see new challenges for growth. He equips and involves people for ministry. He sees people as families and groups rather than as individuals. He emphasizes evangelism, outreach, and starting new units.

Preparing to Launch

Preparation for launching a mission congregation should occur several months before the launch date. Several items need attention:

1. Have the pastor in place.

2. Secure a meeting place.

3. Designate workers to lead the music, teach Sunday School, play the instruments, usher, and provide other ministries.

4. Gather Sunday School and worship service materials. This includes Sunday School literature, hymnals, chairs, musical instruments, preschool equipment, and other items.

5. Plan publicity.

- Ask newspapers and radio and TV stations to cover the event—the birth of a church.
- Send news items to radio and TV stations, newspapers, and denominational publications.
- Prepare a special mail-out inviting community people to the launch service.
- Use the telephone to call all community residents who participated in cultivation activities. In fact, a good publicity package is to link telephone calls with direct mail to area residents. This is very effective in getting people to come to a new church. Several telemarketing methods are available. (See appendix N.)
- Invite demoninational leaders at least three months in advance.
- Invite community leaders, including the mayor, Chamber of Commerce president, and ministerial association chairperson.
- Ask the core group to invite neighbors and other friends.

6. Set the launch time. A Sunday afternoon gives people who are regularly involved in other churches an opportunity to attend without missing their own services. The Sunday School and worship may take place on Sunday morning, with an afternoon launch service in order to give wider participation.

7. Plan the launch service. A sample launch service agenda is shown in appendix O. Mission congregations could adapt the sample to fit their special needs.

Members, Money, and Maturity

The goal of the mission congregation at this point is to reach people for Christ, help them mature in the faith, and develop their stewardship. It should carry out the Great Commission by helping people come to the right relationship with Jesus Christ and grow as disciples. It will practice baptism as commanded in Matthew 28:19. It will seek to develop disciples to be leaders and workers to carry the load of responsibility in the future.

The mission congregation will seek to become self-supporting. For a limited time, it may receive financial assistance from its denomination, sponsoring churches, or other outside sources. But it will seek to become responsible for supporting itself. Peter Wagner says start-up costs for a new congregation are about $60 per member of the mission. He advises planning so the new congregation provides the needed money.[3]

Starting Right

Certain principles and practices built in from the beginning of a congregation's life can keep it from plateauing early or dying.

A primary principle is to **make outreach evangelism a top priority.** Saturating everything with evangelism is a characteristic of growing churches. Evangelism is not just a church program. It is a goal of the choir, the Sunday School, and every church action. Outreach should be the focus of every person in the congregation.

Starting new units should be a high priority. A new unit might be a new Sunday School class, a new men's organization, a new mission organization, or a softball team that would become a bridge into the church. Form a new unit when there is a ministry need and enough workers to lead the unit.

The older a church becomes, the more difficult it is to form new units. People have a tendency to become comfortable and reject change. A new congregation is likely to be more flexible.

A third principle of new church growth is **pastoral ministry style**—the way the pastor does ministry. Starting with the right ministry style can help a pastor avoid a traumatic adjustment later. A pastor who does all of the hospital visitation will be unable to continue when the church nears one hundred in participation. If others start helping with hospital visitation, members may complain that the pastor doesn't visit like he once did.

When the pastor helps people become involved in church ministry, he avoids this problem. He should start training people as they join the church.

A good way to involve people in ministry is to set up a system to help people discover their spiritual gifts. This assists them in knowing and finding their own direction in ministry. It reduces competitiveness in church work. It involves more people at the level where they are capable of service. Church members find fulfillment and become more content in the church if they are exercising their spiritual gifts. They are also more effective in performing a ministry.

A number of pastors ask people to look around and find ministries they think they would like to do. They help them get involved in a particular ministry. This approach seems better than placing people in positions they may not be able to fill.

A fourth principle is **developing a positive attitude.** This is vital to young church growth. As mentioned in a previous chapter, some congregations exercise the grasshopper complex. This is another way of saying they have low self-esteem. It is vital for a new congregation to have a good self-image. Members' positive attitudes will be apparent to those whom they reach for the new church. Steve Dunkin says, "A church never will become more than it perceives itself to be."[4]

A new church has a short history. It may have no prominent members. It may be small. People of the community may ask, "Will it last? Will it stay?" Therefore, church members must express a strong attitude of faith—that they are doing what God wants, and that it will succeed. The pastor and church leaders should do everything they can to foster a good self-image, and it should be reflected in their attitudes. Do things that succeed, even though they may be small. Then when success comes, be sure to compliment the members and celebrate the triumph. Every success will build toward a good attitude for the future. Church members will begin to develop a "can do" attitude and spirit.

Worship is one of the best ways to build an attitude of faith and high esteem. Through worship, individuals recognize God as the supreme authority in life and give Him the honor and praise. Inspiration comes to a congregation when members recognize that they serve a God for whom nothing is impossible. God does not need a huge multitude to accomplish great things. He can take Gideon's army of three hundred and be victorious over thousands. He can part the waters of the Red Sea. He can even raise the dead.

The members of a new congregation should be taught and led to project a positive attitude of faith in visitation and personal contacts with friends and neighbors. The person who is very negative about a new church is a detriment to the group. His attitude and actions can defeat growth, even kill the church start.

The fifth principle of growth for a young congregation is to **provide space** for meeting and parking. The only exception would be inner-city churches or multihousing communities that are within walking distance for most participants.

In most cases, parking space is vital to the growth of the congregation. Purchasing land and erecting buildings becomes a problem for new congregations. This is especially true in metropolitan areas where land is at a premium, building codes are strict, and construction is expensive.

Today's churches must consider alternative meeting places. Some churches have rented space in shopping centers as temporary meeting places. Because of convenient parking, high visibility, and generally acceptable locations, more churches may need to consider shopping centers as permanent meeting places. Westminster Baptist Fellowship in Westminster, California, bought and remodeled a supermarket located in a shopping center. Several churches that meet in shopping centers are growing.

Other alternatives include multiuse of church buildings. Eleven congregations meet in the facilities of Nineteenth Avenue Baptist Church in San Francisco. A central committee handles scheduling and arrangements. Each congregation pays a monthly fee. A central board screens congregations that apply to meet in the building.

Westside Baptist Church in Los Angeles leases meeting space to six congregations. The church is not a sponsoring church to these congregations, though it sponsors two missions in other communities. A board owns the building and leases it out to churches that want to use it.

Participating denominations provided funds for the construction of Interfaith Center, a facility in Columbia, Maryland, where four congregations now meet.

In some rural areas, mobile chapels may be used successfully in beginning a congregation. Double-wide units can accommodate up to one hundred people.

> The most successful arrangement is for the association of churches or state denominational organization to own the mobile unit. The new mission can pay according to its ability. When that congregation no longer needs the unit, it can be moved to service other starting groups. Units that have been moved three times by age eight are still in good condition.
>
> Mobile chapels do have limitations. They can only serve for limited

growth. It may be necessary to have two services. The mobile chapel would not be acceptable in all communities. It is a temporary arrangement that may cause people to wonder if the new congregation is also temporary. This can be overcome by purchasing property. It is risky for the local congregation to purchase the mobile unit. It is not very usable as a permanent part of the building. Construction and zoning codes are problems in some areas.[5]

School buildings also provide possible meeting places. They are usually at well-known locations. Plenty of parking space is available. In most cases, a new church can afford the rental fees. Some school boards welcome churches that want to start in their buildings because of the economic help to the school system.

In many communities, property purchase is a vital step toward a church's establishment in the community. In many areas, particularly smaller towns, land is affordable and available in desirable locations for church buildings. Purchasing land says to the citizens, "This new church means to stay and be a part of the community." It becomes a stabilizing effect in the minds of the people in the area. News will spread fast.

Even though the new congregation may meet in a less-than-desirable location with less-than-ideal arrangements, people will be patient and continue attending if they know a building is planned. The congregation may want to post its building plans or sketches on a prominent bulletin board so that anyone attending can see the church plans to build. The congregation will tolerate many inconveniences as they look forward to a new building.

A rule of thumb in building is that if the church expects to become self-supporting, the first unit of the building should accommodate at least 120 people. Anything smaller than this will not allow for a congregation large enough to support a building program, pastor, and ministry.

Many churches have found it good strategy to build religious education space before building a sanctuary. The church should develop a master plan that may have three different building steps involved. This keeps the congregation from becoming bogged down with heavy debt, while providing acceptable growing space. For a fuller discussion on meeting places, see Lyle Schaller's *44 Questions for Church Planters*.[6]

The sixth principle that affects growth of a new congregation is its **relationship to the community or group.** This relationship may be built during the cultivation stage, as noted earlier. However, the relationship may need renewal and development along the way.

A seventh principle relates to **the way the new congregation treats new people.**

- Welcome them with warm personal greetings.
- Do not single them out during worship by asking them to stand and give their names.
- Avoid an *us* vs. *you* attitude.
- Ask everyone to complete registration cards or registry pads passed down the rows.
- Have a welcoming committee direct newcomers to Sunday School classes and worship services. Meet their needs courteously and quickly.
- Use the term *friends* rather than *visitors* or *guests*.
- Contact first-time visitors by telephone within two days of their attendance. Write a letter within four days. If a visit is appropriate, make it before the next Sunday.

Worship should be exciting, open, nonjudgmental, and have music that targets unchurched people. It should be well planned, but not rigid. Do not assume people know the routine. It should be upbeat and relevant to life.

Group Dynamics

Many of the principles of group dynamics apply to the congregation during the mission stage. This stage in the new church's life cycle builds a vital foundation for future growth. During the mission stage, the congregation moves from a cell group to a core group. Leaders are tested. When the mission approaches the time to become a church, some leaders may be dropped and new leaders elected. Communication becomes more difficult. The group is large enough to form committees to do a lot of background work. No longer can all details be shared with the whole group. Some people may feel they are losing control. Many changes will occur in business meetings and in the ways people are recognized and affirmed. Small groups become more important.

Considering Constitution

As the congregation grows spiritually, numerically, and financially, it will begin to consider constituting from a mission congregation into a church. The sponsoring church and the mission should concur that the mission is able to stand on its own.

Questions to help determine readiness for constitution are:

- Does the mission have enough members to do the basic work without help from the outside?
- Do the members have enough money to carry the financial responsibility of the congregation?
- Is the mission mature and stable in its biblical beliefs?

Timing is important to constitution. If a church constitutes too soon, it may be a weak congregation for many years. If it is held back from constituting when it is ready, it may become discouraged, despondent, or dependent. Usually, when a mission is constituted into a church it becomes revitalized. It is a good time for growth. The constitution event may say to the outside community that this new congregation has made significant development and is definitely a part of the community.

8 GROWING UP

The Church Stage

Several events mark entrance into adulthood. Do you remember when you learned to drive and received your driver's license? Or the first time you drove the car alone? I remember teaching our children to drive. I especially remember when a family member drove one of our cars into the other. The insurance company was not happy.

High school graduation also marks a turning point from youth to adulthood. We never think we know more in life than on the day we complete high school.

College may be a milestone toward adulthood. Moving out "on our own" is another passage into adulthood.

Several achievements may signal a congregation's growth into adulthood. The group may add members, start new ministries, or build a church building. But constitution into a church is the celebration point that speaks most clearly to its members and to the community. Constituting indicates the church's success to the community in which the church is located. It indicates establishment.

Constitution of a new church demonstrates growth and the ability of a congregation to stand on its own. It shows a degree of maturity. And it usually shows goal achievement. It also serves as a springboard for growth. Therefore, the constitution of a church is an important event in the life of a congregation.

A word of caution. A church moving from the mission stage to the church stage may face stringent opposition. Other religious groups or community interest groups may oppose the new church. That opposition surfaces now because the congregation may not have seemed significant enough to contend with before. When constitution comes, the opposition assumes this is a formidable force after all.

Constitution Service

Many of the things written about the launch service for a new mission could be repeated about the constitutional service for a new church. The service should be planned well in advance. For other related reminders, see chapter 7.

Constitution differs from launch in the necessity to handle legal matters. The church property may be held in the name of the sponsor. Any indebtedness built by the mission congregation may also be in the sponsor's name. All bank accounts, deeds, loans, and other legal documents should be transferred to the new congregation. The actual transfers occur after the constitutional service. In reality, the new church does not exist until it votes to constitute. (A sample motion to constitute and sample constitution service appear in appendix P.)

A part of the service may include the adoption of a constitution and bylaws. Some churches may want to ratify articles of faith and a church covenant. Most denominations have samples of statements their churches usually embrace.

A congregation should consider approving a ministry or mission statement. This statement would answer several questions: What kind of church are we? What is our church style? Who is the target group we wish to reach? What kind of church have we become? For what ministries do we feel gifted?

Adjustments for Growth

In order to grow, the congregation first needs to "redream the dream." Perhaps the congregation has reached many of its initial goals. For example, the mission may have hoped to have a fully funded minister. That hope may now be realized. Perhaps they dreamed of enough income to meet their own obligations and do their own ministry without outside assistance. And they have done so.

A young mission pastor said to me, "We accomplished our first dreams, now what do we do?" One approach might be to invite an outside church growth consultant to help identify the strengths of the congregation and lead the people in setting a course. With the assistance of the consultant, the church could establish objectives and goals for the future. Many denominations have church growth programs which can help a young congregation at this stage.

The congregation should take a serious look at its church community or people group. Has the community changed since the mission began? Have new needs been discovered? Is the congregation now large enough to meet needs that it could not handle before?

Several important steps should be taken. First, the pastor must share his personal vision for the church with the people. The pastor cannot carry out the dream alone. Successful pastors include the congregation in realizing the dream. Planning committees can gather data and make recommendations. However, *all* of the members should have the opportunity to share what they think their church should be and do. People who help set goals are more likely to work toward reaching those goals.

Peter Wagner gives five characteristics of good goals:

1. Relevant.—Base goals on research.
2. Measurable.—Establish a time frame and a measuring instrument.
3. Significant.—Goals should make a difference.
4. Manageable.—Goals should be within reach.
5. Personal.—The people should set the goals.[1]

A second important step is the assessment of church leadership needs. Are there enough leaders? Is there a need to develop and involve other leaders? Harry Fowler says a church "must have a leadership structure that involves 60% of the adult members in a task, role, or leadership responsibility."[2]

A third necessary adjustment is a change in the method of recognizing people. A new congregation may recognize birthdays, anniversaries, and other events in the worship service. As the church grows, recognition of all events becomes time consuming. Sunday School departments or other small groups in the church may assume the recognition of many personal events.

Fourth, the church must adjust to its multicelled status. Not all of the members can participate in discussions and know detailed information about every decision the church makes. The church must delegate research and groundwork to small committees, task forces, or other designated groups. These groups gather the information and bring a recommendation back to the church. The church makes the final decision but depends on smaller groups to gather details.

A fifth needed adjustment, especially when church participation is about one hundred, is adding new staff to carry the load. This will ideally handle growth toward the next one hundred members.

The most desirable position to add is an administrative assistant. This person may do some secretarial work but also perform staff responsibilities.

Part of the staff load might be carried by volunteers. For example, a person taking early retirement may have expertise in church functions. This person may be a dedicated, committed Christian willing to serve as a part-time volunteer staff person. However, the main role of staff is to equip lay people to do the work of the ministry.

The minister also needs to begin giving more of the ministry away. Jack Redford says, "My time was eaten up doing things which should have been of low priority. With the three volunteers, I was able to do things which had a higher priority: evangelistic visitation and sermon preparation."[3]

One pastor can carry most of the load of church work until about one hundred people are involved in the church. If the church is to continue to grow, other people must share the load. If the pastor does not share responsibility, he may burn out, leave the church, or become a bottleneck; and the church will plateau at this size.

Growth Observations

In one eighteen-month period, I had the privilege of visiting one hundred new congregations. The following twelve characteristics are common to the growing congregations among them.

(1) The **preaching and teaching ministry is Bible-centered.** Church members say such things as, "Our preacher really preaches the Bible." "My Sunday School teacher feeds me from the Scriptures." "Our Bible discussions are rich."

(2) **Worship with a quality of celebration.** There is a spiritual aliveness. People show their joy in being together to worship God. There is a freedom about worship. People are not inhibited. It is not unusual to hear a spontaneous testimony. Worshipers feel free to go to the platform and ask to share an experience. There is give-and-take between the speaker and audience.

(3) **People are involved,** although the churches are led by staff. New Christians are involved at different levels. One church in Chicago meets in a school building. People come as early as 7:00 a.m. to begin setting up equipment and getting ready for Bible study and worship. People in these churches are involved—leading in prayer, singing, giving testimonies, taking care of physical arrangements, serving refreshments, and greeting others.

(4) Another common element is **small-group meetings.** Most of them emphasize Sunday School. The Sunday School classes are small, caring groups in which people pray for one another and share concerns.

Some new congregations have groups that meet in homes during the week. These small, caring groups minister to one another's needs. Members of the group become accountable to one another. They also serve as outreach groups that draw new people into the circle.

(5) **Spiritual maturation** takes place. Various methods are used for this. Some churches have Discipleship Training on Sunday nights before worship services. Others have classes for new Christians and new church members. Some have nurturing systems in which

they pair new Christians with more mature Christians. Southern Baptist churches often use the *Survival Kit for New Christians*.[4]

These churches teach people how to pray, study the Bible, have a daily maturing fellowship with Christ, and grow spiritually. They teach the meaning of serving in Jesus' name. They teach and encourage stewardship and giving.

(6) The next common element is the **attitude of faith.** Positive attitudes show. The church members in growing churches are satisfied customers. They project positive attitudes as they talk with others. They are enthusiastic about the future of their churches.

Charles Chaney writes,

> The church is called to victory, to growth, and to the multiplication of units. A church whose members believe that under God they can, can! One of the most essential factors to proper mental preparation for church planting is a spirit of faith, victory, and confidence permeating the congregation and its leaders. A church that expects great things from God can attempt great things for God.[5]

(7) These churches hold a **vision from God.** Members look forward to the future with excitement. They feel God has done something through their congregations and plans to do great things in the future. It is a shared vision described by both the congregations and ministers.

(8) Pastors of these congregations **work hard and smart.** They don't just do things, they do the right things to make the church grow. They concentrate on meeting spiritual needs of members and discovering unchurched people. They work on outreach and ministry that meets felt needs.

(9) These churches also **lift up, encourage, and enrich the family.** They are aware that families need a great deal of help and are tuned in to assisting and helping families. Most of these churches recognize the changing family in our day. Many minister to single parents with children and give special attention to singles.

(10) The churches **relate well to the needs and interests of**

the community. They don't just do any kind of ministry. They find out what the people need and desire and meet some of those needs.

(11) These churches do **high quality programs and ministry.** They don't try to do everything. But what they do, they do well.

(12) The final observation about these churches is that they **have strong pastoral leadership.** I do not mean they have domineering pastors. Pastoral leadership styles vary (democractic, free-reign, autocratic, independent, relational, and casual).[6] But the pastors know what is going on and have a sense of vision and direction. They actively lead the church. The pastors know their people and their communities. They understand their leaders, know what has succeeded and what has failed, and have plans and a vision for the future. To grow or not to grow is not an option with them. They center on growth. People who want to grow with them are encouraged to join.

Paul was a strong leader. In 1 Corinthians 3:6, he acknowledges that God gave the increase. But he did not disclaim his active role in the results of planting. Ted Engstrom says, "The Christian leader must also recognize his personality and gifts, the needs of the people, and the given condition. He cannot be driven by the thirst for power."[7]

This list of growth principles is not intended to be complete. These are simply observations of characteristics of some new and growing churches.

THE LIFE CYCLE BEGINS AGAIN   9

Why should a congregation that is perhaps very young consider sponsoring another congregation? Some of the reasons appear below.

(1) It **is biblical.** Jesus was unselfish, serving, and obedient to the Father. Jesus said, "Upon this rock I will build my church; and the gates of hell shall not prevail against it" (Matt. 16:18). The church was in the mind of Christ. Donald McGavran says it succinctly, "Church multiplication was an essential part of New Testament life."[1]

Jesus started the church. Parent churches practice Philippians 2:5, "Let this mind be in you, which was also in Christ Jesus."

The church has always been God's plan for carrying out the Great Commission. It has proved to be the best way to evangelize and minister to people, and for Christians to grow and serve Christ.

(2) Church planting **is unselfish.** When a church begins to center upon itself, it inevitably begins to die spiritually. Spiritual vitality grows as a church reaches out and establishes new congregations in other places. It is following Jesus' command to take the gospel to all people. Jack Redford says, "The cutting edge—the point of thrust in missions—is church starting. To be involved in church starting is to be at the very heart of mission endeavor."[2]

Missiologist Jim Montgomery says,

> As I have tried to demonstrate, multiplying churches until a country is filled with them is not only good theory and theology for the discipling

of a nation. It also is demonstrably the best and fastest way to grow and make disciples. All strategies for world evangelization and all methods of evangelism, in my estimation, need to so design their ministries that the planting of new churches is at least one primary outcome.[3]

(3) Church planting **attracts committed people** to the sponsoring church. Many people join a church because they find it to be unselfish. People want to be part of a church that is reaching out to extend the gospel beyond its own walls. The people in sponsoring churches seem to have a high degree of commitment. They want to serve and reach others with the good news of Christ's love.

(4) Church planting **contributes to stewardship of money** in the sponsoring church. Interviews in Arkansas churches indicate that sponsoring churches had more tithers and larger offerings than the average Baptist church in the state. Perhaps this was a reflection of the commitment of the people.

(5) Church planting **promotes a higher quality and quantity of growth in the sponsor.** The quality of growth refers to the commitment mentioned above. It is the spiritual maturity of members. Quantity of growth has to do with additions and baptisms. "The average Baptist church in Arkansas baptized nine people in 1986. Churches that sponsored missions baptized 32 people."[4]

(6) Church planting **gives continuity.** Inherently, people want to keep their names alive. They want the ideals and characteristics which they hold dear to be perpetuated. A sponsoring church experiences that thrill. A new mission will continue to carry out the Great Commission. C. Peter Wagner says, "The single most effective evangelistic methodology under heaven is planting new churches."[5]

(7) Church planting **provides new blood.** Lyle Schaller says, "Historically new congregations have turned out to be the most effective approach to reaching new generations of people."[6]

People have a life cycle that carries them through death. Churches seem to experience growth, a plateau, and, in most cases, eventual decline. If a church declines, how can it continue to carry out the

Great Commission? Of course, the answer is a new offspring. New congregations abound with fresh energy, new ideas, and current methods for reaching a modern generation.

Starting a new congregation does not just perpetuate the old church. It reaches into a new generation. A new congregation can recognize new circumstances and changes in society while holding firm to the principles and truths of the Word of God. Changed methods and approaches often get the maximum response from a new generation. This is urgent business. The Princeton Religion Research Center reports that 73 percent of 1,067 unchurched adults interviewed indicated they would want their children to receive religious training.[7]

A new-church start, like the birth of a new baby, brings some natural rewards to parents. But the greatest motivation for planting is biblical. It is an unselfish way to continue carrying out the Great Commission through a new generation.

Planting a new congregation gives the older congregation a major goal to live for. It is an exciting new adventure in reproduction. Sometimes terminally ill grandparents hold on a little longer just to see a new baby. A grandchild rejuvenates many a grandparent. New churches rejuvenate and extend the arm of the family tree.

A new congregation also reaches into the unchurched population. Sixty percent of the people who join a new congregation were not previously active in a church.

Charles Chaney says,

> When we asked the question about greatly multiplying the number of churches, we were addressing a question that is at the heart of the missionary task of the Church of Jesus Christ. We focused on the crucial, specific activity upon which the evangelization of America—in all of its cultural and social complexity—depends.[8]

In summary, planting new churches is biblical, practical, historical, pragmatic, strategic, exciting, and productive.

10 CHURCH PLANTING PARADIGMS

A midwife attended my birth at home. A doctor delivered our son at a hospital. Birthing centers provide facilities for the births of babies today. People generally follow the birthing paradigm (model or pattern) of their day.

This chapter contains ten church-planting paradigms. In the 1990s church planters should use these models in the proper settings.

The Nontraditional Congregation

The term *nontraditional congregation* means different things depending upon denominational usage. Nontraditional must be defined within the context of what is traditional for a particular faith.

Over an eighteen-month period, I visited fifteen nontraditional congregations located in California, Georgia, Illinois, and Kansas. The following comments are not a scientific survey. They are simply deductions from my observations of these churches.

Several questions need to be answered related to the nontraditional congregation.

(1) What comparison makes the congregation nontraditional? Is it compared to other congregations of its own denomination? Or is it compared to the Christian faith?

(2) What is nontraditional about the congregation? Is it the method of approach, such as meeting times, music style, and organizational structure? Or is it scriptural teachings?

(3) Are the beliefs and practices of the congregation biblically based?

(4) Is the pastor a stable, maturing Christian leader?

(5) Are the core-group leaders biblically sound?

(6) Is the new church cooperative with its wider fellowship of believers?

(7) Does the congregation seem to have a biblical vision of what the church should be and do?

(8) Are any basic scriptural principles being compromised?

Answering these questions can help a religious organization that is linked to a nontraditional congregation determine whether the nontraditional group holds solid, biblical beliefs.

Two conditions in the 1990s make nontraditional approaches desirable ways to reach some people. Many people born in the United States since 1960 do not have church backgrounds. We cannot expect them to know the hymns or be familiar with the Bible. These unchurched people may respond more readily to churches that use contemporary Christian music with the words printed or on overhead projection.

Second, the nontraditional approach can target a people group that needs a new church. Worship styles may be adapted to their needs. The church can be "user friendly" and "customer responsive." Starting a church from the standpoint of the needs and interests of the target group helps a new congregation get maximum response to the gospel.

Jack Redford reports a good response to a nontraditional chapel service when he was a chaplain. Redford says,

> I had a nice choir, nice robes, good sermons, I thought, but like the preachers from the other denominations, I couldn't get anybody to come. Something was wrong. So, one day, I decided to change my style. I dismissed the choir and hung up their nice robes in a closet, and found a guitar player and hired a revival preacher because I didn't know how to preach that way myself anymore. In no time, my chapel was

overrun. I couldn't stand the service myself, but the thing is, you just have to respect the cultural, economic and intellectual level of the people you want to reach.[1]

Another question arises about nontraditional churches. Should the denominational name be included on the sign and printed materials? Some church leaders say omitting the name is not being completely honest with the unchurched. On the other hand, some church planters say including the denominational name blocks some people before the church has the opportunity to relate to them. I think the answer must be determined by the individual situation.

Do nontraditional churches progress through the same basic stages of the life cycle as described in this book? My observations are limited to fifteen nontraditional congregations at this time. But these groups are proceeding through the usual stages.

Successful Telemarketing in a New Church

Each year Southern Baptist church planters use telemarketing to start about seventy churches. Some positive things about the telemarketing approach make it desirable.

(1) Telemarketing helps a few people make a large number of contacts.

(2) Telemarketing helps build a mailing list of unchurched people.

(3) Telemarketing usually enables a new congregation to begin with a larger group than other methods produce.

(4) Telemarketing helps allay fears of other ministers and church members in the area. The new church can convey its intent to target the unchurched.

(5) Telemarketing gives general publicity of a new congregation's beginning in the area.

However, telemarketing does have several disadvantages.

(1) In some areas people have reacted adversely to telemarketing. In these areas, using it for church planting can create a negative attitude toward a new congregation.

(2) Telemarketing alone does not develop a solid congregation.

(3) Telemarketing may be more expensive than some new congregations can afford.

Urban Church Planting

In 1790, only 5 percent of the people in the United States lived in urban areas.[2] The figure rose to 51 percent by 1920 and in 1991 was an amazing 76 percent.[3]

The number of churches is not proportionate to the population. For example, only 43 percent of Southern Baptist churches are located in urban areas where 77 percent of the people reside.

Adjusting from rural to urban living is not easy. Life in rural areas or small towns centers on the people. Urban society is performance oriented. Rural is homogeneous; urban is diverse. Values in the rural community tend to be mutually accepted. In urban areas, pluralistic values coexist. The rural neighborhood is relatively static; the urban is characterized by change. Family includes immediate and extended units in rural areas. An individual is accepted as a family in urban areas. Diverse people groups and types of communities exist in one urban area.

Urban church planters must face several issues in the 1990s. First, the church planter needs a clear picture of the people who need a church. How many are there? What are they like? What are their needs and interests?

Second, sponsors need better preparation to mother urban missions. The expectation of the sponsor should match the potential of the new congregation.

Third, the church-planting approach should be adapted to the characteristics of each community. An inflexible approach will not work for all new starts.

Fourth, success for a church may need to be redefined. Churches are needed in inner cities where buildings are not available. Success cannot be measured by baptisms, budgets, and buildings. The people may be very mobile. The church may exist only a few years or even months.

Fifth, the larger fellowship of faith must learn to accept different styles of churches.

Sixth, people need to see the church as people, not buildings.

Seventh, support groups must learn to fund new congregations adequately without making them dependent churches.

Eighth, sponsors must provide support systems for urban workers so they will not bomb out, bail out, or burn out.

Lay Church-Planting Team

Several Baptist associations have formed teams of volunteers to start congregations. Team members come from several churches. These bivocationals work at secular jobs but give time to starting congregations.

Members of the team commit themselves to the new congregation for six months to a year. Some of them stay and become permanent members of the new congregation. The latter is likely to occur if the team member lives in the community where the new congregation is beginning.

Included on a lay team are the team members needed as initial workers for a new mission launch. Remember: team members should be compatible with the target group.

Bivocational Church Planters

During the westward movement in the United States, many new churches were started by people who made their living in secular vocations such as farming, carpentry, and ranching. Sometimes a group of people requested a certain person to lead in starting a congregation. Some church starters had already felt called to the ministry. Most of the people who served as bivocational church starters were also moving west.

Today many ministers make their living at other vocations while serving as pastors of churches. In most instances, the minister does secular work because the church is too small to provide full support.

In the 1990s, many bivocational church planters are needed. Some may begin churches in which they continue to serve as pastors. Other bivocational church planters will start churches, grow them to the point of calling fully supported pastors, and move to other communities to begin the process again.

The ideal is for the bivocational pastor to come from the local community or people group.

The Revitalized Church

First Baptist Church of Houston, Texas, has taken on a special ministry of revitalizing churches. Harry Kneisel, minister of missions, coordinates the revitalization efforts. Last year, First Baptist worked with seventeen missions and four mission fellowships.

In some instances revitalizing a congregation really means planting a new church. Many of the churches are in changing communities. Most of an old congregation may have moved, leaving a few members and the building. First Baptist, Houston, provides financial assistance, workers, and guidance to develop a church in the existing facility. Community residents become part of the church. The church takes on the characteristics of the community. In some cases more than one congregation meets in the same building.

Multihousing Congregations

Starting congregations inside multihousing communities is new for most churches in America. This is discussed more fully in chapter 3.

First Baptist Church of Marion, Arkansas, started a mission in Lakeshore Estates among twelve hundred manufactured-home residents. The church met in a mobile chapel on a corner lot. In its first two years the church received seventy-two people by baptism.

First Baptist Church of Arlington, Texas, sponsors more than one hundred missions. The majority are in multihousing locations.

The Key Church Plan

In the key church plan, a church calls a minister of missions to serve on its staff.

An annual goal for the minister of missions is to lead in beginning at least five congregations. The new congregations may be predominantly African American, ethnic, or Anglo. They may be located in multihousing communities, single-family suburbs, or other locations.

A key church is usually located in an area where a large number of new congregations is needed. However, a strong church in one state may sponsor a minister of missions in another state or area where multiple new starts are needed. The key church holds the mission congregation's membership and records its attendance figures.

The Moving Target Church

Twenty percent of the U.S. population moves each year. Some communities and housing patterns such as apartment complexes and manufactured-home communities have a rapid turnover—as much as 30-50 percent in a year. Churches composed largely of people from military bases are illustrations of these kinds of congregations.

Pastors of high-turnover congregations sometimes near despair. They reach people who become active in the church. Then these people transfer or move to other communities. Pastors and leaders must then enlist and train new people.

This movement of people can be a positive thing. For example, persecution came upon the church at Jerusalem and Christians were scattered. They shared the good news of the gospel wherever they went (see Acts 8:1-8). As a result of Christians leaving Jerusalem, churches were started in many other areas (see 11:19-21).

Why not challenge the people who are leaving congregations to be missionaries as they go? Churches could commission these people and send letters recommending them for church planting. They might become core groups for new congregations in their new locations.

Some people move to another apartment complex. They might

become the core family for a new congregation in that complex. Those moving to other military bases may find the need for new congregations near their new homes.

Two Are Better Than One

"Two are better than one, because they have a good return for their work: If one falls down, his friend can help him up. But pity the man who falls and has no one to help him up!" (Eccl. 4:9-10, NIV). Many times when a congregation starts in an area, the pastor and workers feel lonely and isolated. Beginning a new congregation differs from working in an existing congregation.

In areas where multiple new starts are needed, two or more may start at the same time. This has proven to be effective in several places.

The pastors of new congregations can have fellowship, learn from one another, and help provide a support system. It is easy for them to share helpful ideas with each other.

Conclusion

I hope you have been able to identify the essential elements that produce a healthy church. This could help you determine if your congregation has completed important stages of development. The Life Cycle Identification Worksheet in appendix Q may help you discover where your congregation is and evaluate its effectiveness. It may be worth the time and effort to go back and strengthen some foundational areas. Here is a quick review of the essentials:

Does your church have a complete picture of the people in its community who need a new church? Could your congregation grow faster if it understood and related to the characteristics and needs of the target group? Does your church have up-to-date demographics and psychographics? Do you need to review this information?

Is pastoral leadership compatible with the unchurched target group? Does the pastor fit the community theologically, sociologically, and in life-style?

Is the core group of the church like the people the church is trying to reach? Do you have enough leaders to produce growth? Is the core group firmly committed to Christ, to one another, and to planting a new church in the community? Some new churches have "borrowed" workers or core group leaders from sister churches in order to get started.

Has your target community been sufficiently cultivated? Does the community know your church cares about them in the name of Christ? Has your church earned the respect of its target group by service and performance? Do the people of the community know about your church and that they would be welcomed? Has your church already met some felt needs?

Has your church developed an identity? Does it have a ministry statement? If not, the church may need to agree on the kind of church it has become and what target group it can best reach.

If your congregation is still a mission, was the sponsoring church prepared to be a good mother? Does your sponsor know it has a child?

Perhaps the relationship needs further endearment. You and your church members could visit the sponsor on special occasions such as revivals. Give a verbal report in their next business meeting. Request prayer for specific mission needs. Write some thank you letters. Invite the sponsor members to visit their mission. Send pictures with your monthly reports. Remember, you will be sister churches some day.

Focus the dream. How long has it been since all mission members have discussed the vision for their congregation? Is it time to share ideas again? Should goals be reshaped?

What about space? When your meeting space and parking is 80 percent full, you have reached maximum capacity. Do you need to rent more space, bring in mobile units, or relocate?

Are your people practicing evangelistic outreach? Do they need training or motivation?

Is your congregation starting new units? Do members know new units are the quickest, least expensive way to grow? Has at least one new unit been started in the last two months?

Leaders and workers are essential to growth. Do you have a steady stream of workers being prepared and developed for growth? Some workers may need rest before they burn out. It is good to detect signs of illness early. Are ailments being treated before they become debilitating diseases?

Is your congregation preparing the nursery for a new baby? The life cycle can keep on going. How many of the thousands of new congregations needed in the United States can your church mother?

NOTES

Introduction

1. Rodney W. Napier and Matti K. Gershenfeld, *Groups: Theory and Experience*, 3d ed. (Boston: Houghton Mifflin, 1985), 458.

2. Floyd Tidsworth, Jr., "Loss of Missions in Six New Work Southern Baptist State Conventions" (Study for Fuller Theological Seminary class project, July 1983).

Chapter 1

1. Dale A. Miller, "The Biological Future of Pest Control," *Vital Speeches of the Day*, Vol. LV, No. 11 (Mount Pleasant, S.C.: City News Publishing Co., 1989), 337.

2. Jack Redford, *Planting New Churches* (Nashville: Broadman Press, 1978), 8.

3. Charles L. Chaney, *Church Planting at the End of the Twentieth Century* (Wheaton, Ill.: Tyndale House Publishers, 1982), 33, quoting Melvin Hodges, *Build My Church* (Chicago: Moody Press, 1957), 97.

4. Chaney, *Church Planting*, 33, quoting J. Terry Young, "The Holy Spirit and the Birth of Churches," in *The Birth of Churches*,

Talmadge R. Amberson, ed. (Nashville: Broadman Press, 1979), 163.

5. See Chaney, *Church Planting,* 21-24.

6. Henry T. Blackaby, *What the Spirit Is Saying to the Churches* (Atlanta: Home Mission Board, SBC, 1988), 33.

7. C. Peter Wagner, *Leading Your Church to Growth* (Ventura, Calif.: Regal Books, 1984), 65.

8. David Putman, "Getting Off to a Big Start," in Charles L. Chaney, *Church Planting at the End of the Twentieth Century* (Wheaton, Ill.: Tyndale House Publishers, rev. 1992), 231-33 in draft copy.

9. C. Peter Wagner, "How to Plant a Church" seminar, 1984 (p. 2), Charles E. Fuller Institute of Evangelism and Church Growth, P.O. Box 90910, Pasadena, CA 91109-0910. Phone: (800) 999-9578.

10. Lyle Schaller, *Growing Plans* (Nashville: Abingdon Press, 1983), 18.

11. Carl F. George, "The Role of New Churches," *How to Plant a Church,* Fuller Seminar, Chicago, 1984, 2.

12. Lyle E. Schaller, *44 Questions for Church Planters* (Nashville: Abingdon Press, 1991), 66.

13. Table: "Status of Churches Organized 1972 to 1982 after Five Years of Existence," Research Divison, Home Mission Board, SBC.

14. See David R. Ray, *Small Churches Are the Right Sizes* (New York: The Pilgrim Press, 1982).

15. Wagner, *Leading Your Church to Growth,* 173.

16. Harry H. Fowler, *Breaking Barriers of New Church Growth* (Rocky Mount, N.C.: Creative Growth Dynamics, 1988), 55.

17. Floyd Tidsworth, Jr., *How to Start and Develop Missions That Become Healthy, Growing Churches* (Little Rock: Arkansas Baptist State Convention, 1984), 20.

18. Napier and Gershenfeld, *Groups,* 460.

19. Robert D. Dale, *To Dream Again* (Nashville: Broadman Press, 1981), 26.

Chapter 2

1. Bruce A. Baldwin, Director of Psych Systems Consultation Service, Wilmington, N.C. Article clipped in 1980; publication unknown.

2. Larry L. McSwain and William C. Treadwell, Jr., *Conflict Ministry in the Church* (Nashville: Broadman Press, 1981), 144.

3. See Avery T. Willis, Jr., *MasterLife* (Nashville: Sunday School Board of the Southern Baptist Convention, 1982). A sequential, group-discipling process that enables one to make Christ Master and to master life through practicing basic disciplines.

4. Quoted by Buckner Fanning, pastor, Calvary Baptist Church, San Antonio, Texas. Audiotape of December 1990 worship service.

5. Kenneth Blanchard and Spencer Johnson, *The One Minute Manager* (New York: The Berkley Publishing Group, 1982), 44.

6. Henry T. Blackaby, *What the Spirit Is Saying to the Churches* (Atlanta: Home Mission Board, 1988), 42.

7. See *American Demographics* (magazine), P.O. Box 68, Ithaca, NY 14851. Telephone (800) 828-1133 ($58 per year for twelve issues).

8. Tidsworth, *How to Start and Develop Missions*, 16.

Chapter 3

1. Bernard Quinn, et al., *Churches and Church Membership in the United States 1980* (Atlanta: The Glenmary Research Center, 1982). An enumeration by region, state, and county based on data reported by 17 denominations, 111 church bodies.

2. See Tidsworth, *How to Start and Develop Missions*, 5.

3. David T. Bunch, Harvey J. Kneisel, and Barbara L. Oden *Multihousing Congregations* (Atlanta: Smith Publishing, 1991), 2.

4. Ibid., 1, 3, 11.

5. George Barna, Conference at Baptist Sunday School Board, Nashville, Tenn., May 5, 1991.

6. Schaller, *44 Questions,* 161.

7. David Putman, "Getting Off to a Big Start" in Chaney, *Church Planting,* Rev. 1992, 236ff. in draft copy.

8. Carol Childress, Gordon Lawrence, and Larry Wartsbaugh, "Harnessing Old and New Technology in Church Planting" in Chaney, *Church Planting,* rev. 1992, 185-87 in draft copy.

9. George Barna, *What Americans Believe* (Ventura, Calif.: Regal Books, 1991), 83-92.

10. Paul W. Powell, *How to Make Your Church Hum* (Nashville: Broadman Press, 1977), 71.

11. John Naisbitt and Patricia Aburdene, *Megatrends 2000, Ten New Directions for the 1990's* (New York: William Morrow and Co., Inc., 1990), 307.

Chapter 4

1. Chaney, *Church Planting,* 18.

2. "Church Arkansas" brochure (Little Rock: Arkansas Baptist State Convention, 1987).

3. C. Peter Wagner, "How to Plant a Church" seminar, 1984 (p. 3), Charles E. Fuller Institute of Evangelism and Church Growth, P.O. Box 90910, Pasadena, CA 91109-0910. Phone: (800) 999-9578.

4. Ebbie C. Smith, *Balanced Church Growth* (Nashville: Broadman Press, 1984), 60.

5. Ibid., 46.

6. Chaney, *Church Planting,* 39.

Chapter 5

1. Redford, *Planting New Churches,* 13.

Chapter 6

1. See Chaney, *Church Planting,* 47-50.

2. Ron Nichols, et al., *Small Group Leaders Handbook* (Downers Grove, Ill.: InterVarsity Press, 1982).

3. C. Peter Wagner, "How to Plant a Church" seminar, 1984 (p. 14), Charles E. Fuller Institute of Evangelism and Church Growth, P.O. Box 90910, Pasadena, CA 91109-0910. Phone: (800) 999-9578.

4. David Putman, "Getting Off to a Big Start," Chaney, *Church Planting,* 1992, 216.

Chapter 7

1. Copyright 1983, Fuller Evangelistic Association. Used by permission. Presented by Robert E. Logan, "How to Plant a Church" seminar, 1984, Charles E. Fuller Institute of Evangelism and Church Growth, P.O. Box 90910, Pasadena, CA 91109-0910. Phone: (800) 999-9578.

2. George, "Selecting Leaders," *How to Plant a Church,* Fuller Seminar, Chicago, May 1984, 684.

3. C. Peter Wagner, "How to Plant a Church" seminar, 1984 (p. 8), Charles E. Fuller Institute of Evangelism and Church Growth, P.O. Box 90910, Pasadena, CA 91109-0910. Phone: (800) 999-9578.

4. Steve Dunkin, *Church Advertising, A Practical Guide* (Nashville: Abingdon Press, 1982), 51.

5. Floyd Tidsworth, Jr., *Planting and Growing Missions* (Durham, N.C.: Moore Publishing Co., 1979), 26-27.

6. Schaller, *44 Questions,* 60.

Chapter 8

1. C. Peter Wagner, "How to Plant a Church" seminar, 1984 (p. 2), Charles E. Fuller Institute of Evangelism and Church Growth, P.O. Box 90910, Pasadena, CA 91109-0910. Phone: (800) 999-9578.

2. Harry H. Fowler, *Breaking Barriers of New Church Growth* (Rocky Mount, N.C.: Creative Growth Dynamics, 1988), 39.

3. Redford, *Planting New Churches*, 24-25.

4. Ralph W. Neighbour, Jr., *Survival Kit for New Christians*, Adult, Youth, and Children's Editions (Nashville: Sunday School Board, SBC, 1979).

5. Chaney, *Church Planting*, 1982, 86.

6. C. Peter Wagner, "How to Plant a Church" seminar, 1984, Charles E. Fuller Institute of Evangelism and Church Growth, P.O. Box 90910, Pasadena, CA 91109-0910. Phone: (800) 999-9578.

7. From the book *The Making of a Christian Leader* by Ted W. Engstrom. Copyright © 1976 by the Zondervan Publishing House. Used by permission.

Chapter 9

1. Donald A. McGavran, 1977, quoted by Chaney, *Church Planting,* 78.

2. F. J. Redford, *Reach People! Start Churches! A Guide for Starting Churches* (Atlanta: Home Mission Board, SBC, 1984), 1.

3. Jim Montgomery, *Dawn 2000: 7 Million Churches to Go* (Pasadena, Calif.: William Carey Library, 1989), 45.

4. "Church Arkansas" brochure (Little Rock: Arkansas Baptist State Convention, 1987).

5. C. Peter Wagner, *Church Planting for a Greater Harvest* (Ventura, Calif.: Regal Books, 1990), 11.

6. Schaller, *44 Questions,* 28.

7. *The Unchurched American — 10 Years Later* (Princeton, N.J.: The Princeton Religion Research Center, 1988), 36.

8. Chaney, *Church Planting,* 18.

Chapter 10

1. C. Peter Wagner, "How to Plant a Church" seminar, 1984

(p. 5), Charles E. Fuller Institute of Evangelism and Church Growth, P.O. Box 90910, Pasadena, CA 91109-0910. Phone: (800) 999-9578.

2. Larry L. Rose and C. Kirk Hadaway, *The Urban Challenge* (Nashville: Broadman Press, 1982), 10, quoting *the Bureau of the Census,* Historical Statistics of the U.S. (Washington, D.C.: U.S. Department of Commerce, 1975), part 1, 12.

3. Larry L. Rose, "Trends Affecting Churches and Associations in the '90s," *Associational Bulletin* (Atlanta: Associational Missions Division, Home Mission Board, Oct.-Dec. 1991).

APPENDIX A

InSite*USA
Demographic and Income Forecast Report*

Area: TRACT/MCD 130670315.00

Summary Profile	1980 Census	1990 Update	1995 Forecast	1990-1995 Change	1990-1995 Ann. % Chg.
Population	11501	16431	17064	633	0.76
Households	3525	5432	5860	428	1.53
Average HH Size	3.26	3.02	2.91	−0.11	−0.76
Median Age	28.5	30.7	32.8	2.1	1.34
Per Capita Income	6941	14296	16302	2006	2.66
Median HH Income	21613	42933	47377	4444	1.99

	1980 Census		1990 Update		1995 Forecast	
Household Income	no.	%	no.	%	no.	%
$ 0 to 14999	965	27.4	649	11.9	641	10.9
$15000 to 24999	1206	34.2	589	10.8	530	9.0
$25000 to 34999	912	25.9	690	12.7	650	11.1
$35000 to 49999	346	9.8	1490	27.4	1344	22.9
$50000 to 74999	73	2.1	1537	28.3	1683	28.7
$75000 and up	23	0.7	477	8.8	1012	17.3

Age Distribution	no.	%	no.	%	no.	%
0 to 4	850	7.4	1136	6.9	1154	6.8
5 to 9	1097	9.5	1226	7.5	1132	6.6
10 to 14	1253	10.9	1270	7.7	1222	7.2
15 to 19	1149	10.0	1481	9.0	1264	7.4
20 to 24	765	6.7	1502	9.1	1471	8.6
25 to 29	921	8.0	1448	8.8	1492	8.7
30 to 34	1149	10.0	1144	7.0	1437	8.4
35 to 39	1032	9.0	1258	7.7	1134	6.6
40 to 44	743	6.5	1381	8.4	1244	7.3
45 to 49	653	5.7	1227	7.5	1359	8.0
50 to 54	468	4.1	872	5.3	1198	7.0
55 to 59	349	3.0	729	4.4	838	4.9
60 to 64	388	3.4	553	3.4	686	4.0

*Copyright 1990 CACI, Fairfax, VA (800) 292-2240. Used with permission.

	1980 Census		1990 Update		1995 Forecast	
Age Distribution	no.	%	no.	%	no.	%
65 to 69	283	2.5	393	2.4	505	3.0
70 to 74	165	1.4	360	2.2	343	2.0
75 to 79	121	1.1	240	1.5	293	1.7
80 to 84	63	0.5	118	0.7	178	1.0
85 and up	52	0.5	93	0.6	114	0.7
Race Distribution	no.	%	no.	%	no.	%
White	10530	91.6	14981	91.2	15519	90.9
Black	906	7.9	1314	8.0	1374	8.1
Other	65	0.6	136	0.8	171	1.0

Important:
1. Household income includes the income of families and unrelated individuals. Household income is the total available income for the area.
2. Income figures are expressed in current dollars for 1980 and 1990. 1995 figures are expressed in 1990 dollars.

APPENDIX B

InSite* USA
ACORN Population Market Segment Report *

Area: TRACT/MCD 130670315.00
Base: United States

ACORN Types   Population

	1990	%	Base %	Index
A 1: Old Money	0	0.0	0.5	0
A 2: Conspicuous Consumers	0	0.0	1.2	0
A 3: Cosmopolitan Wealth	0	0.0	2.1	0
B 4: Upper Middle Income Families	0	0.0	3.3	0
B 5: Empty Nesters	0	0.0	2.6	0
B 6: Baby Boomers with Families	3570	21.7	4.3	511
B 7: Middle Americans in New Homes ..	2246	13.7	5.6	245

ACORN Types	Population			
	1990	%	Base %	Index
B 8: Skilled Craft & Office Workers	0	0.0	4.4	0
C 9: Condominium Dwellers	0	0.0	1.6	0
C 10: Fast Track Young Adults	0	0.0	5.0	0
C 11: College Undergraduates	0	0.0	0.8	0
C 12: Older Students & Professionals	0	0.0	1.4	0
D 13: Urbanites in High Rises	0	0.0	0.9	0
D 14: Big City Working Class	0	0.0	1.1	0
E 15: Mainstream Hispanic Americans ...	0	0.0	2.6	0
E 16: Large Hispanic Families	0	0.0	2.0	0
E 17: Working Class Single Adults	0	0.0	1.1	0
E 18: Families in Pre-War Rentals	0	0.0	1.1	0
E 19: Third-World Melting Pot	0	0.0	0.9	0
F 20: Mainstream Family Homeowners ..	0	0.0	3.5	0
F 21: Trend Conscious Families	0	0.0	1.8	0
F 22: Low Income Families	0	0.0	0.9	0
G 23: Settled Families	1343	8.2	3.8	213
G 24: Start-Up Families	6913	42.1	5.9	711
H 25: Family Sports & Leisure Lovers ...	0	0.0	2.2	0
H 26: Secure Factory & Farm Workers ...	0	0.0	2.0	0
H 27: Family Centered Blue Collar	0	0.0	3.4	0
H 28: Minimum Wage White Families	2359	14.4	4.3	336
I 29: Golden Years Retirees	0	0.0	2.0	0
I 30: Adults in Pre-War Housing	0	0.0	4.4	0
I 31: Small Town Families	0	0.0	5.9	0
I 32: Nostalgic Retirees & Adults	0	0.0	0.9	0
I 33: Home Oriented Senior Citizens	0	0.0	1.7	0
I 34: Old Families in Pre-War Homes ...	0	0.0	4.1	0
J 35: Resort Vactioners & Locals	0	0.0	0.8	0
J 36: Mobile Home Dwellers	0	0.0	1.1	0
K 37: Farm Families	0	0.0	0.7	0
K 38: Young, Active Country Families ...	0	0.0	0.3	0
L 39: Low Income Retirees & Youth	0	0.0	3.1	0
L 40: Rural Displaced Workers	0	0.0	0.1	0
L 41: Factory Worker Families	0	0.0	2.7	0
L 42: Poor Young Families	0	0.0	0.6	0
M 43: Military Base Families	0	0.0	0.9	0
M 44: Institutions: Residents & Staff	0	0.0	0.3	0
Total	16431	100.0	100.0	

APPENDIX C

InSite*USA
ACORN Population Cluster Group Report*

Area: TRACT/MCD 130670315.00
Base: United States

ACORN Groups

	1990	%	Base %	Population Index
A: Wealthy Metropolitan Communities	0	0.0	3.8	0
B: Trend Setting, Suburban N'hoods	5816	35.4	20.2	175
C: Apartment House & College Areas	0	0.0	8.8	0
D: Big City Urban Neighborhoods	0	0.0	2.0	0
E: Hispanic & Multi-Racial N'hoods	0	0.0	7.7	0
F: Black Neighborhoods	0	0.0	6.2	0
G: Young Middle Class Families	8256	50.2	9.8	515
H: Blue Collar Families in Sm. Towns	2359	14.4	11.9	120
I: Mature Adults in Stable N'hoods	0	0.0	19.0	0
J: Seasonal and Mobile Home Commun ..	0	0.0	1.9	0
K: Agriculturally-Oriented Commun	0	0.0	1.0	0
L: Older, Depressed Rural Towns	0	0.0	6.4	0
M: Special Populations	0	0.0	1.2	0
Total	16431	100.0	100.0	

APPENDIX D

Community Survey Sheet

Name of Area Surveyed _____

Person(s) Interviewed _____

Address _____

Telephone ( ) _____

Ask these questions:

1. What do you think are the needs in this community? _____

_____

*Copyright 1990 CACI, Fairfax, VA (800) 292-2240. Used with permission.

2. What do you feel a church can do to help meet these needs?

_____

3. Can you give the name of a person living in the area who has a special need not being met?

Name _____

Need _____

Address _____

Telephone _( )_____

Person Conducting Survey _____

Telephone _( )_____

Date of Interview _____

APPENDIX E

Community Needs and Prospect Survey

Resident's name _____ Sex ___ Date _____

Address _____ Phone _____

"Hello, (Mr./Mrs. ____). My name is ____ and I am assisting _____ with a survey of households in this community on religious activities and views. The interview takes only a couple of minutes, and you may skip any questions you prefer not to answer. Will you help us?"

(If the resident agrees to help, complete the interview. If resident refuses, thank him or her graciously and leave.)

"First, a few questions about your family's religious activities:

1. About how often does your family attend church? Would you say weekly, once or twice a month, seldom, or never?

___ Weekly   ⟩

            ⟩ Go to No. 2

___ 1-2 Month ⟩

___ Seldom   ⟩

___ Never   ⟩ Go to No. 3

___ Don't know ⟩

2. Where does your family attend church? _____

3. Does your family have any religious preference? _____

4. In your opinion, what are some specific needs within this community? _____

_____

"Now, just a few questions about your own religious view. Again, you may skip any question you prefer not to answer."

5. In your opinion, why do many people no longer attend church today? _____

_____

6. Would you want a child of yours to receive religious instruction?
Yes ___ No ___ No children ___ Don't know/not relevant ___

7. Would any members of your family attend a new church in this community?
Yes ___ No ___ Don't know/not relevant ___

8. How important would you say religion is in your own life? Would you say it is very important, fairly important, or not very important?
Very ___ Fairly ___ Not very ___ Don't know/not relevant ___

9. (Confirm name of interviewee:) _____

"Thank you for your help."

Interviewer's name _____

For incomplete survery, check:

___ Refused (couldn't talk)

For incomplete telephone survey, check:
___ Wrong number

___ Refused (wouldn't talk)

___ No one home,
(date) _____

___ No household member
home, (date) _____

___ House vacant (moved)

___ New construction (not
occupied)

___ No answer (1st attempt),
(date) _____

___ No answer (2nd
attempt), (date) _____

___ Busy, call back

___ Phone not in service

___ Moved

APPENDIX F

Area Analysis Form

City _____ State ___ County _____	Paste up or sketch map of target area.
Area's Name (Description of area in adjacent map)	
Name of Person Completing this Analysis	
1. RELIGIOUS DATA (Source: Personal Interviews, Telephone Yellow Pages and Observation)	

(1) How many unchurched are in this area?

Unchurched	Number	*Percent
(Your denomination) preference		
Other preference		
Total		100%
Names and addresses in hand		
Have expressed interest		

* Calculate by dividing total into number in each group.

_____ Miles

(2) What percentage of the people in the area attend religious services?

Weekly   Monthly   Seldom   Never

(3) Does any church attempt to reach this area now? How?

(4) If previous attempts to start a church in this area failed, why?

(5) Nearest church (of your denomination):

1) How many miles is it from target community?   2) Is this church compatible with the kind of church that should be started in this area?

(6) What church is logical to sponsor new work?

(7) Denominations represented in the area by name and membership:

	Number Members	Number Attendants	Number Churches		Number Members	Number Attendants	Number Churches
Your Denomination				Methodist			
Catholic				Lutheran			
Jewish				Assembly of God			
Episcopal				Nazarene			

2. POPULATION DATA (Resource: 1990 Census and Planning Commission)

(1) What is the current population of the area by the ethnic and age groups listed below?

Ethnic/Culture Groups			Age Groups		
Types	Number	Percent	By Years	Number	Percent
White			0-17 years		
Black			18-34 years		
Hispanic			35-54 years		
Asian			55-64 years		
European			65 and over		
Other			Total		

	1960	1970	1980	1990	2000 (Projected)
(2) Population					

3. ECONOMIC DATA (Resource: Local office of state employment agency; planning commission)

(1) Describe the area economy (agriculture, manufacturing, mining, government installations and institutions, military, commerce and trade, tourism, recreation)

(2) What are the five largest job classifications represented in the area? (manufacturing, agriculture, construction, transportation, trade, finance, service, mining, government)

(3) What percentage of the people are in each of the following categories?

Employment Groups	Percent	Income Groups	Percent
Executive, administrative and managerial		Less than $10,000	
Professional specialty		$10,000-14,999	
Health technologists and technicians		$15,000-24,999	
Technologists and technicians except health		$25,000-34,999	
Sales occupations		$35,000-49,999	
Clerical and administrative support occupations		$50,000 and Over	
Service occupations		(4) Type of Community	
Farming, forestry, and fishing occupations		☐ New Town ☐ Open Country ☐ Transitional ☐ Suburban ☐ Exurban (Rural Urban) ☐ Small Town ☐ City ☐ Inner City	
Production and maintenance occupations		ACORN Readout (3 largest categories) Number of people Percentage	
Other		_____ _____ _____ _____ _____ _____	

(5) What are current housing trends in this area?

	Occupancy	Number	Percent	Type Housing	Units	Percent
Owner				* Single family		
Renter				* * Multifamily		
				Mobile home		
Total			100%	Total		100%
				* 1 unit in structure * * 2 or more units		

(6) Educational attainment (%)	Elementary	High School	Prof./Tech.	College	Graduate

APPENDIX G

Church Budget Worksheet

Congregation's Name _____

Budget Items	Amount Budgeted
MISSIONS	
World Missions	
National Missions	
Local Missions	
STAFF SUPPORT	
Pastor's Salary	
Housing	
Travel	
Annuity	
Insurance	
Convention Expense	
Cleaning Coordinator	
Secretary	
Other	
MINISTRIES	
Sunday School	
Vacation Bible School	
Discipleship Training	
Music	
Youth	

Church Budget Worksheet (continued)

Budget Items	Amount Budgeted
Local Mission Units	
Revivals	
Pulpit Supply	
Literature	
Other	
BUILDING	
Payment	
Insurance	
Maintenance	
Cleaning Supplies	
Rent	
Utilities	
Other	
OFFICE EXPENSES	
Bulletins	
Equipment	
Postage	
Supplies	
Other	
TOTALS	

APPENDIX H

Church Starting Planning Form*

Target Area/Community _____

City/State _____ Association _____

Sponsoring Church _____

1. Population/Demographics

	1980	Current	Projected 1990	Projected 2000
Number	_____	_____	_____	_____
Percentage Increase	_____	_____	_____	_____

2. Preparation Plans/Actions
(What will we do?)

	Date (When?)	Responsibility (Who?)	Resources (Costs?)
Sponsoring-Church Leaders			
Sponsoring church committed	_____	_____	_____
Missions Development Council selected	_____	_____	_____
_____	_____	_____	_____
Church Preparation			
Films/special services	_____	_____	_____
Missions presentations	_____	_____	_____
Series of messages	_____	_____	_____
Training programs	_____	_____	_____
Prayer emphasis	_____	_____	_____
Commitment service	_____	_____	_____
Start-a-Church Commitment Sunday	_____	_____	_____
_____	_____	_____	_____
Prospect Surveys			
Sample survey	_____	_____	_____
Telephone	_____	_____	_____

*James L. Hill, Associational Church Extension Guide (Atlanta: Home Mission Board, SBC, 1989), 39.

Door-to-door _____ _____ _____

_____ _____ _____ _____

_____ _____ _____ _____

Cultivation Plans

Complete surveys _____ _____ _____

Regular visitation _____ _____ _____

VBS/Back Yard Bible Clubs _____ _____ _____

Community activity _____ _____ _____

_____ _____ _____ _____

_____ _____ _____ _____

Fellowship Period

Leadership/curriculum _____ _____ _____

Meeting places _____ _____ _____

Joint fellowships _____ _____ _____

_____ _____ _____ _____

_____ _____ _____ _____

New Church Launch

Arrange meeting places/facilities _____ _____ _____

Select relational guidelines _____ _____ _____

Organize Sunday School/officers _____ _____ _____

Plan worship service _____ _____ _____

_____ _____ _____ _____

_____ _____ _____ _____

Total Cost (prior to launch): _____

3. **Church Planter/Mission Pastor/Contact Person**

Name _____ Phone _____

Address _____

City/State/Zip _____

4. **Mission Plans and Goals**	At Launch	6 Months	First Year	Second Year
Sunday School Attendance	_____	_____	_____	_____

Number of units (1-18) _____ _____ _____ _____

Number of workers (1-8) _____ _____ _____ _____

Sunday School Enrollment _____ _____ _____ _____

Worship Service Attendance _____ _____ _____ _____

Membership _____ _____ _____ _____

Baptisms _____ _____ _____ _____

Average Offerings _____ _____ _____ _____

Projected annual offerings _____ _____

5. Projected Budget Plans and Funding Sources

(Complete and attach a projected budget worksheet for first two years.)

Funding Sources (monthly amounts):

Need	Year	New Church	Sponsor	Partner	1	2	3	4	5	Association	State	HMB	Total

Mission Pastor Support Package

___ ___ ___ ___ ___ ___ ___ ___ ___ ___ ___ ___ ___ ___

___ ___ ___ ___ ___ ___ ___ ___ ___ ___ ___ ___ ___ ___

___ ___ ___ ___ ___ ___ ___ ___ ___ ___ ___ ___ ___ ___

___ ___ ___ ___ ___ ___ ___ ___ ___ ___ ___ ___ ___ ___

Purchase Church Site

___ ___ ___ ___ ___ ___ ___ ___ ___ ___ ___ ___ ___ ___

___ ___ ___ ___ ___ ___ ___ ___ ___ ___ ___ ___ ___ ___

___ ___ ___ ___ ___ ___ ___ ___ ___ ___ ___ ___ ___ ___

___ ___ ___ ___ ___ ___ ___ ___ ___ ___ ___ ___ ___ ___

Construct First Unit Building

___ ___ ___ ___ ___ ___ ___ ___ ___ ___ ___ ___ ___ ___

___ ___ ___ ___ ___ ___ ___ ___ ___ ___ ___ ___ ___ ___

___ ___ ___ ___ ___ ___ ___ ___ ___ ___ ___ ___ ___ ___

___ ___ ___ ___ ___ ___ ___ ___ ___ ___ ___ ___ ___ ___

Special Projects

1 ___ ___ ___ ___ ___ ___ ___ ___ ___ ___ ___ ___ ___ ___

2 ___ ___ ___ ___ ___ ___ ___ ___ ___ ___ ___ ___ ___ ___

3 __ __ __ __ __ __ __ __ __ __ __ __ __ __ __

4 __ __ __ __ __ __ __ __ __ __ __ __ __ __ __

Total
Funds: __ __ __ __ __ __ __ __ __ __ __ __

Note: All figures are monthly amounts for calendar years. The sponsoring church (Sponsor) and the partnershp church (Partner) are long-term commitments for the five years of the project. Assisting churches may make short or long-term commitments. The monthly total should be adequate to meet the attached Church Budget Worksheet projections.

Completed by _____ Date _____

APPENDIX I
The Mission Fellowship Leader

1. Qualifications
   (1) A person of unquestionable dedication to Christ
   (2) A person of solid biblical conviction
   (3) An active church member
2. Relationships
   (1) Work in cooperation with the larger fellowship of believers.
   (2) Communicate with immediate supervisors, the church missions council, and sponsoring-church pastor.
3. Actions
   (1) Receive training provided for mission fellowship leaders.
   (2) Become familiar with the assigned field.
   (3) Develop the mission fellowship.
   (4) Encourage the sponsoring church to elect a missions council.
   (5) Work with the missions council and pastor in matters related to the mission fellowship community.
   (6) Secure homes for prayer and Bible study meetings.
   (7) Conduct Bible study and prayer meetings in homes.
   (8) Coordinate the work of volunteers for the mission fellowship field.
   (9) Develop a complete survey of the field. Set up an active file

listing names, addresses, and telephone numbers of the unchurched.

(10) Visit unchurched people.

(11) Visit prospects and report progress and needs to the sponsoring church.

(12) Lead people to Christ.

(13) Train people to work in the new mission. Give attention to volunteers' motivation and attitudes.

(14) Prepare for the launch of the mission congregation.

(15) Assist the sponsoring church in securing a pastor for the mission congregation.

4. When the mission is ready to call a pastor, the association may ask the mission fellowship leader to accept another mission assignment.

APPENDIX J
Sample Commissioning Service

Hymn	"Send the Light"
Prayer	
Welcome and Recognitions	
Hymn	"Set My Soul Afire"
Scripture	Romans 10:12-15 or Isaiah 6:1-13
Offering	
Mission Testimony	
Special Music	"People to People"
Message	
Invitation	

(Invite all who plan to work in or attend the mission congregation to come forward for dedicatory prayer and remain for congregational greetings.)

Responsive Reading	(See sample below.)
Dedicatory Prayer	
Hymns	"Tell the Good News"
	"Reach Out and Touch"
Closing Prayer	

Sample Responsive Reading

Pastor: "Then I heard the voice of the Lord saying, 'Whom shall I send? And who will go for us?' And I said, 'Here am I. Send me!'" (Isa. 6:8, NIV).

Congregation: "As it is written, 'How beautiful are the feet of those who bring good news!'" (Rom. 10:15, NIV).

Pastor: "Therefore go and make disciples of all nations, baptizing them in the name of the Father and of the Son and of the Holy Spirit, and teaching them to obey everything I have commanded you. And surely I am with you always, to the very end of the age" (Matt. 28:19-20, NIV).

Congregation: "But you will receive power when the Holy Spirit comes on you; and you will be my witnesses in Jerusalem, and in all Judea and Samaria, and to the ends of the earth" (Acts 1:8, NIV).

Pastor: "We are therefore Christ's ambassadors, as though God were making his appeal through us. We implore you on Christ's behalf: Be reconciled to God" (2 Cor. 5:20, NIV).

Congregation: "For this reason, since the day we heard about you, we have not stopped praying for you and asking God to fill you with the knowledge of his will through all spiritual wisdom and understanding" (Col. 1:9, NIV).

Pastor: "Do not be anxious about anything, but in everything, by prayer and petition, with thanksgiving, present your requests to God. And the peace of God, which transcends all understanding, will guard your hearts and your minds in Christ Jesus" (Phil. 4:6-7, NIV).

APPENDIX K

Sample Relationship Agreement

Good communication is the key to good relationships. The sponsoring church shall appoint a church missions council to work with the mission congregation's steering committee or council. It will be the responsibility of the two councils to develop and maintain good communication between the sponsoring church and the mission congregation.

In reality, the mission congregation is the church. It is simply the church meeting in a different place. It is the church extended. The mission congregation shall be governed by the constitution of the sponsoring church in all matters that pertain to it.

I. Relationships

    A. The mission congregation and the sponsoring church shall agree on the person to call as pastor of the mission congregation.

        1. A committee of five—three members from the mission congregation and two members from the sponsoring church—shall be elected as a pulpit committee.

        2. The prospective pastor shall be asked to speak before both congregations and be voted on by both.

    B. The new congregation pastor shall move his church membership to the sponsoring church.

    C. The mission congregation pastor and the sponsoring-church pastor shall agree on evangelists to invite for mission congregation revivals.

II. Church Membership

    A. Mission congregation members can be received according to the sponsoring church's constitutional membership provisions. After accepting a candidate's request for church membership, the mission congregation shall submit the candidate's name to the sponsoring church for vote and baptism or to obtain a church letter.

III. Business

    A. Any ordinary business items related to the mission congregation's work may be transacted by the mission congregation. Business items that directly involve the sponsoring church should be presented to the sponsoring-church clerk one week prior to the church's monthly business meeting. In no case will the mission congregation become indebted without the sponsoring church's approval.

B. The mission congregation shall submit a written report of all mission congregation business, attendance, and growth to the sponsoring church at its monthly business meeting.

C. The mission congregation shall be in contact with the sponsoring-church missions council on matters of business and meet with the council as needed for reports and other communication.

D. The mission congregation may observe the ordinances of the church upon approval of the sponsoring church.

IV. Tithes and Offerings

A. All tithes and offerings shall be kept by a treasurer, elected by the mission congregation and approved by the sponsoring church. The treasurer shall make a monthly report of all receipts and expenditures.

B. The mission congregation shall support world missions.

C. The mission congregation shall designate a percentage to national missions.

D. The mission congregation shall designate a percentage to local missions.

V. General

A. The mission congregation shall use the Bible.

B. The mission congregation shall use program materials designated by the group with which it is affiliated.

C. When the sponsoring church and/or the mission congregation determine that the mission congregation is strong enough to organize into a New Testament church, they should express this to the missions council. In business session, the missions council should recommend, for church and mission congregation action, that the mission congregation constitute as a church.

D. The sponsoring church shall do all in its power to enable the mission congregation to be the church God intends it to be. Prayer for the mission congregation is essential. The church shall be available for spiritual guidance, counsel, and assistance in visitation. The mission congregation shall pray for, love, respect, and cooperate with the sponsoring church for the mutual blessings of both.

Sponsoring Church Approval Date _____

Signed _____

(pastor/moderator/church clerk)

Mission Congregation Approval Date _____

Signed _____

(pastor/moderator/mission clerk)

APPENDIX L

Two Personality Tests

1. Myers-Briggs Type Indicator

   Developed by I. Myers in 1962 to measure bipolar dimensions of personality. The Myers-Briggs is a personality assessment measure for ascertaining how persons perceive and judge. The four primary dimensions measured are:

   (1) Extroversion vs. Introversion: whether a person's attention is directed to people and things or to ideas.

   (2) Sensing vs. Intuition: whether a person prefers to perceive information by the senses or by intuition.

   (3) Thinking vs. Feeling: whether an individual prefers to use logic and analytic thinking or feelings in making judgments.

(4) Judgment vs. Perception: whether an individual uses judgment or perception as a way of life. That is, does the individual evaluate events in terms of a set of standards or simply experience them?

About one hour is needed to complete the inventory. Scoring can be done manually or by machine.[1]

2. California Psychological Inventory (CPI)

H. G. Gough developed the CPI in 1957. Its purpose is to give a description of a normal personality. In other words, it is to test personality in "normal" people, rather than diagnose mental illness. Fifteen personality scales are used to test these areas:

(1) Dominance
(2) Capacity for status
(3) Sociability
(4) Responsibility
(5) Socialization
(6) Tolerance
(7) Achievement via conformity
(8) Achievement via independence
(9) Intellectual efficiency
(10) Psychological mindedness
(11) Femininity
(12) Social presence
(13) Self-acceptance
(14) Self-control
(15) Flexibility[2]

---

[1]R. S. Arulis, *Encyclopedia of Psychology,* Raymond J. Corsini, ed. (New York: John Wiley and Sons, 1984), 2:414.

[2]Richard J. Lanyou and Leonard D. Goodstein, *Personality Assessment,* 2d ed. (New York: John Wiley and Sons, 1971, 1982), 84-88.

APPENDIX M*
Specialized Function of:

CATALYZERS (CATS)	ORGANIZERS (ORGS)	OPERATORS (OPS)
Can start a group from scratch, attracting people and other resources.	Can take a jumble of pieces and design an orderly organization, maximizing resource utilization.	Can keep an organization going, if main assumptions and philosophy of ministry are not changed.
Tend to become frustrated when size of group begins to require more amount of time and energy or organizational maintenance.	Tend to lose challenge when original disorder is under control.	Tend to be frustrated when disorder goes beyond normal levels.
As mature, may leave organization or recruit organizer, operator teammates or drop out from frustration.	As mature, may opt for benefits of operator style.	As mature, tend to become unaware of how growth occurs and becomes defensive in presence of growth-oriented people.
These types are rare enough to be in scarce supply.		These types soon become a majority.
In business, valued and compensated highly as entrepreneurial type.	In business, organizers often advance by changing jobs. They often build upon the work of entrepreneurs.	Operators tend to gain control of ongoing systems and *if not aware* of value of Catalyzers and Organizers will overvalue themselves to the extent of discrediting and criticizing the types who preceded them. When such attitudes prevail, Catalyzers and Organizers may exit to build new para-church organizations.

APPENDIX N
Telemarketing

TeleReach Manual: Using the Telephone to Reach People (5270-34) and *Get in Touch . . . Keep in Touch: A Sunday School Outreach Communication Plan* (5270-30). *Get in Touch . . . Keep in Touch* outlines a way to contact new homeowners within zip code areas. Names are available through Broadman Prospect Services. The plan includes sample survey forms, telephone procedures, and follow-up letters. These items are available from Baptist Book Stores.

The Phone's for You is a telemarketing program with sample conversations and letters for contacts during a nine-week period. For information, contact Church Growth Development International, 420 W. Lambert, Suite E, Brea, CA 92621, (714) 991-9621.

APPENDIX O
Sample Launch Service

Hymn
Scripture Reading
Welcome and Recognition of Visitors
Introduction
Missions Council Statement
> (Missions council gives reasons a church is needed in the community.)

Sponsoring-Church Affirmation
> (The sponsoring-church pastor affirms the new church, assuring members of the sponsoring-church's support.)

Presentation of Mission Congregation
> (Presider presents people involved in the mission congregation and announces locations and times of mission's regular meeting place.)

Hymn
Special Music
Message
Invitation

    (Invite people to become members of the new mission.)
Reception and Fellowship

APPENDIX P

Sample Motion to Constitute

Whereas, We believe there is a need for a (your denomination) church in this community, and

Whereas, After prayer, we believe we have found God's divine guidance, and

Whereas, We have consulted with fellow Christians and neighboring churches, and

Whereas, We have called a council to consider this matter, and the council has recommended we proceed with the constitution of the new church,

Resolved, That we enter into the organization of a _____
    Church.

Sample Constitution Service

Hymn
Scripture Reading
Prayer
Reading of the Mission Congregation's History
Welcome and Guest Recognition
Statement of Meeting's Purpose
Recommendation to Constitute

    (The sponsoring church recommends that the mission congregation constitute.)
Vote to Constitute

    (Members of the new church vote. The new church is born at this point.)
Adoption of Church Covenant
Adoption of Articles of Faith, Constitution, and Bylaws
Vote to Affiliate

    (Vote is unnecessary, if the constitution states that the church is affiliated with its community of faith.)
Recognition of Charter Members
Election of Officers

(A nominating committee should present names of moderator, clerk, pastor, teachers, and other officers.)
Sponsoring Church Vote
(Sponsor votes to recognize the new congregation as a constituted church.)
Special Music
Message or Charge to New Church
Invitation for New Members
Offering
Benediction
Right Hand of Fellowship to Members of the Newly Constituted Church
Fellowship Time

APPENDIX Q

Life Cycle of a New Congregation

Identification Worksheet

CONGREGATIONAL STAGES	DISCOVERY	PREPARATION	CULTIVATION	FELLOWSHIP	MISSION	CHURCH
(My Congregation)						
AGE PERIODS	1 to 6 months	1 to 3 months	2 to 4 months	2 to 18 months	1 to 5 years	
(My Congregation)						
GROUP STAGES				Cell	Core	Congregation
(My Congregation)						
ORGANIZATIONAL STAGES				Start-up	Organization	Growth
(My Congregation)						
SIZE				6 to 60	30 to 120	60+
(My Congregation)						
PLATEAU SIZES		30 to 40	60 to 75	80 to 120	120 to 150	175 to 200
(My Congregation)						